Dogs Bark, but
the Caravan Rolls On

March 25, 2002
Iowa City

To Nancy

with much love –

Frank

Books by Frank Conroy

STOP-TIME

MIDAIR

BODY & SOUL

DOGS BARK, BUT THE CARAVAN ROLLS ON

Dogs Bark, but the Caravan Rolls On

Observations Then and Now

Frank Conroy

HOUGHTON MIFFLIN COMPANY

Boston • New York

2002

For information about permission to reproduce selections from
this book, write to Permissions, Houghton Mifflin Company,
215 Park Avenue South, New York, New York 10003.

Visit our Web site: www.houghtonmifflinbooks.com.

Library of Congress Cataloging-in-Publication Data
Conroy, Frank, date.
Dogs bark, but the caravan rolls on : observations
    then and now / Frank Conroy.
    p.   cm.
ISBN 0-618-15468-X
    I. Title.
PS3553.05196 D64 2002
814'.54—dc21   2001051884

Book design by Melissa Lotfy
Typefaces: Minion, Perpetua

Printed in the United States of America

QUM 10 9 8 7 6 5 4 3 2 1

The following stories also appeared, in slightly different form, in these publications: *Esquire:* "My
Generation," "Marsalis at Twenty-three," "The Serkin Touch," "Scouts' Honor," "The Basic Impera-
tive"; *GQ:* "Father," "Running the Table," "My Teacher," "My Harlem," "Great Scott"; *Parenting:*
"Father Thoughts"; *Glamour:* "A New Father," "The Mystery of Coincidence"; *Harper's Magazine:*
"Think About It"; *New Times:* "Jarrett"; *New York Times Magazine:* "Hip Vaudeville," "Marsalis at
Thirty-four."
    "The Writers' Workshop" previously appeared in *On Writing Short Stories*, edited by Tom
Baily; "Small-Town America" in *Small Town America: The Missouri Photo Workshops, 1949–1991*,
edited by Cliff and Vi Edom and Verna Mae Edom Smith; "Me and Conroy" in *Who's Writing
This?*, edited by Daniel Halpern; "Leaving New York" in *Leaving New York: Writers Look Back*, ed-
ited by Kathleen Norris.

For the elders
Hanne, Ellen and India

And the newcomers
Nicholas and Jonathan

ACKNOWLEDGMENTS

I want to thank Larry Cooper for his help. He sees what others do not see, and hears what others do not hear. My thanks also to Neil Olsen for his patient support.

Contents

A Note on the Title

I CAN'T REMEMBER where I first saw the aphorism "Dogs bark, but the caravan rolls on." Some years ago in a book, perhaps, addressed to a writer whose work had been trashed by a reviewer. At lunch with Malcolm Bowie, the critic and Oxford don, I wondered aloud at its provenance. He held his knife and fork aloft and looked into the middle distance. "Proust used it, I think." A pause. "From the *Arabian Nights*, maybe." A month later he sent me the relevant pages from *À la Recherche du Temps Perdu,* with a note that one of his reference books defined its meaning as, "People may carp, but carpers are soon forgotten." It is possibly an Arabian proverb. The reference-book meaning seems fine, if brief. Proverbs often have a kind of elasticity, which may be why they are proverbs to begin with.

The observer as dog. I've got no problem with that—I've had seven dogs in my life and was fond of them all. The one I have now seems particularly intelligent, comports herself with dignity and can read minds (at least the minds, on occasion, of myself and my wife). Useful characteristics, certainly, for any writer attempting to observe the world and scribble something down. No problem with "dogs."

The "bark" is where it starts to open up. Watchdogs bark to announce the possibility of a threat of some kind on the periphery of their territory. There are writers, journalists and reviewers who seem spurred by similar motives—to protect the sanctity of art from the barbarians, even if the barbarians are artists. I like to think I haven't done this.

There is another kind of bark, of course, many different kinds of barks, as dog people know. The ordinary dog's bark of excitement, the bark of eagerness, interest and anticipation— these seem especially appropriate in terms of what I imagine myself to have been doing writing about this and that, one thing or another, all these years.

It would be nice to have the original proverb in its original language. All the difference in the world between "*and* the caravan . . ." and "*but* the caravan . . ." In the former the dogs might be celebrating the forward movement, in the latter perhaps trying to arrest it. In any event, I take it the dogs are asserting themselves. The caravan is time flowing endlessly on, while the dogs bark from specific points of time. The caravan is mysterious, with who knows what inside the closed wagon.

I say "wagon" because almost forty years ago I lived in England, in a cottage in Surrey near the large house where Constance Garnett had done her translations from Russian. Behind my cottage was a thickly wooded hillside, which I would sometimes explore. Late one afternoon I came across a faint but definite track deep in shadow. I sat on a rock to rest, and after a few moments a closed black wagon pulled by a single horse emerged silently from around a curve. It was followed by a man on foot, followed by other silent wagons and silent men, none of whom so much as glanced at me. Gypsies. A Gypsy caravan moving through the woods.

2001

*Dogs Bark, but
the Caravan Rolls On*

Some Observations Now

I N 1968 a pal of mine who worked for *The New Yorker* was sent to cover the Democratic convention in Chicago. During the infamous police riots he was struck two or three times by a cop with a nightstick, and when he managed to get back to his hotel he found himself pissing blood. He eventually recovered, wrote his piece and left out the attack on himself. "Michael," I asked my always elegantly dressed, highly polite friend, "how could you leave it out? You weren't protesting. It shows the scope of the violence. It's important." He respectfully disagreed. "I wasn't sent to write about myself," he said, with a certain amount of hauteur. New Journalism was in the air back then—an approach in which the observer was taken to be as important, or more important, than the stuff observed (Tom Wolfe, for instance, writing about auto shows, well before taking on the more ambitious role of American Balzac). *The New Yorker* frowned on New Journalism. People took sides. I never did, whether from laziness or a reluctance to box myself in, I don't know. I dealt with each piece I wrote as seemed appropriate at the time.

The closest I came to New Journalism was probably a long piece (endlessly long, in fact) about the late movie star Steve McQueen, written for what was then considered not the best but the hippest magazine around, *Esquire*. McQueen, whom I had never thought much of as an actor, turned out to be a nice guy. Unassuming, straightforward, easygoing if a touch wired, he was good company. We had fun riding 250 cc dirt bikes in the desert around Palm Springs, drinking beer, eating Mexican food at out-of-the-way joints and swimming in the pool behind his Palm Springs house, his getaway pad (his mansion was in Beverly Hills, of course). It was my first "big" magazine piece. Still in my twenties, I was thrilled by the whole experience. I left something out of my piece, though, something I knew the editors would probably like, and, so too, the readers. On my third visit to his house—"Come over for lunch," he said, "around eleven"—he surprised me.

It was an ordinary suburban neighborhood, and I drove into the circle at precisely eleven A.M., parked the car and rang his front door bell. After a long time the door opened. McQueen, his entirely naked body wet and gleaming, peeked out at the street and then looked at me. "Come on back to the pool."

Was he showing off? His body was flawless, front and back, and quite beautiful. One did not have to be gay (and neither of us was) to be moved by its perfection. Was he saying he had nothing to hide to a writer who would, he knew, be writing about him? Was he asserting his freedom to do whatever he wanted to do—the kid from the orphanage who grew up to be a movie star? Was it an expression of trust? Who knows? Perhaps he just didn't think it was that important.

He lent me a pair of trunks, though, because he didn't know when his wife and kids would be back.

Writing for money. Not very much money, to be sure, but I did it occasionally. (My first book, *Stop-Time*, had been a critical success, but brought in next to nothing.) *The New Yorker* had printed chapters from my book, and Mr. Shawn, who ran the place, suggested I might want to try a "Notes and Comment" now and then. I wrote a dozen or so over the next couple of years, but finally stopped because I overreacted to rejection. Whenever he turned one down, even with good reason, it broke my heart. (In my teaching I emphasize that a writer must learn how to deal with rejection, and must never be weakened or slowed down because of it. I have dealt with it badly myself, so I know what I'm talking about.) I also overreacted to acceptance. Once I wrote a short story in a single go, nine hours of continuous immersion which left me manic and exhausted. Mr. Shawn bought the story and printed it a week later. I wasted a month celebrating.

Magazines had once been an important part of American culture. Hemingway's *Old Man and the Sea* was first printed in *Life*, read by millions of people. The *Saturday Evening Post, Collier's* and others published fiction in every issue, thousands of stories a year, lots of nonfiction, and thus supported all kinds of writers. Television ended that era, but when I was young we still read what was left pretty faithfully. *The New Yorker* was important to us. As my drinking buddy Terry Southern used to say, "It's the top of the quality-lit biz."

One night I walked into a favorite literary hangout and sat down with Willie Morris, the flamboyant editor of *Harper's Magazine*. Charles Manson had just been arrested and the whole country was agog. "Who's going to do Manson for *Harper's*?" I asked, genuinely curious. Willie was, of course, drunk. "You are," he said immediately. "You are. You."

I thought it was the booze talking, but he asked the waiter for some paper and wrote out a contract on the spot. We both signed, and two waiters signed as witnesses, and Willie bought a round of drinks. A month later I delivered the article, a "think piece" as they used to call them at *The New Yorker*, which Willie liked well enough to make the cover story. A terrific editor, who knew when to simply let a writer go.

Some editors were insupportable. A young guy at one of the

bigger "slicks" asked me to go out to California and do a story on Anouk Aimée, the ethereally beautiful French actress who'd hit it big with a movie called *A Man and a Woman*. "She's going to see Disneyland, according to her PR guy." I accepted the assignment, spent three or four days with Anouk and her guitar-playing boyfriend, went to Disneyland with them, came back to New York and wrote an article. It was hard work. Anouk was indeed beautiful, but a dim bulb. A soul under water, really. I thought I captured a certain poignancy in her situation, but the editor killed the piece. "I was thinking of the irony of it," he said. "You know, French sophistication against the vulgarity of Disneyland." In other words, he had a piece in mind despite the fact that he'd never met Anouk Aimée and never been to California. A few experiences of this kind taught me to be very careful about assignments. I backed off from magazine work almost entirely, in fact, earning money doctoring movie scripts instead. (Cleaning up dialogue, mostly, for princely sums. It didn't seem to matter whether the producers made the movie or not. But I began to hate the work itself—the movies were stupid—and eventually the well went dry.)

Years later, after my marriage had ended and I left New York to live in the boondocks, broke, jobless and confused, I was to look back with mild alarm at how casual I'd been about money, how spoiled I'd been by a decade of modest income from my trust funds (which ran out) and my wife's (which, thank God, did not), wrapped in a comfortable fog of well-being. The cliché is true: when you don't really need money, it's easy to get, and when you absolutely must have it, it's hard to come by— particularly if you've left town. New Yorkers tend to think of anyone who's left as having died. They simply forget about you. For quite some time I scrabbled around, playing the piano at jazz bars, doing whatever pickup journalism I could get. I was grateful when an acquaintance at the *New York Times Magazine* called long distance to ask if I wanted to do a piece on the Rolling Stones. "You bet," I said. "Thanks."

I knew nothing about rock, never listened to it except in passing on the car radio and had no interest in it. (The Beatles were another story. I bought all their records and even played a few of their tunes with my trio.) I had to ask my twenty-four-year-old girlfriend, "Who are the Rolling Stones? I mean, I've heard of them, but what's the big deal?"

She looked at me suspiciously, as if I'd started playing some unspecified word game. "You mean you really don't know?"

"No."

"Does the name Mick Jagger ring a bell?"

"He's in the group, right? He sings?"

(Let me digress with another note about New York. My male pals understood me well enough to know I couldn't live alone—indeed, I tried it for a year, housesitting in Connecticut and feeling very, very sorry for myself—and many of them argued that I should stay in the city because I'd never find a woman in the boondocks. They were wrong, as New Yorkers are so often wrong about the outside world. The twenty-four-year-old girlfriend who proceeded to tell me all she knew about the Rolling Stones eventually married me, and is still with me thirty years later. We have a fifteen-year-old son who listens to Tony Bennett.)

Once again I was to leave something out of the story. I had no choice, really, given the venue. But I can tell it here. The Rolling Stones were about to begin an American tour, and had rented Andy Warhol's estate at the northern tip of Long Island to go over their repertoire. Flashing my coded telegram at various checkpoints, I arrived at a sprawling one-story house with wings in all directions. I found a door, knocked and, after some time, simply entered. To my left, an enormous kitchen. "Hello? Anybody home?" I moved past the entrance hall and through an arch on my right to what looked like a large, informal living room. "Hello?" Complete silence. It was around four o'clock in the afternoon.

I sat down on a couch, feeling a bit nervous, and flipped through some magazines from a side table. After perhaps three quarters of an hour I got up and walked over to the French windows, stared out at the lawn and came back again. On the other side of the room were amplifiers, mike stands, stacks of speakers, a drum set, cables on the floor and a Steinway baby grand. I sat down at the piano and played some Thelonious Monk. Then some Jaki Byard. I got into it, as they say—concentrating. I played the blues, and suddenly the sound of the drums came from behind my back. Crisp, light ride cymbal, steady high hats and short riffs on the snare, echoing little licks from my right hand. Classic jazz drums, something like Kenny Clark. I just kept on playing when a bass joined in, completing the trio with a swinging four-to-the-bar walking line. It sounded so good to me I couldn't stop, and we must have done fifty choruses. Finally I played the head to "Blues in the Closet," lifted my hands and turned around.

"Hey," said the skinny guy behind the drums. "I've played with you before." This was Charlie Watts, the Stones' drummer, but I had never seen the group and didn't recognize him.

"I—uh, well," I mumbled.

"The Establishment!" he said. "Back in the old days."

Ah, yes. London. A nightclub with a downstairs jazz scene where the house pianist, Dudley Moore, let me sit in now and then. (This was before rock hit England, when Gypsy caravans might be spotted in the countryside.) "Right," I said. "Good Lord."

Charlie introduced me to Bill Wyman, the bassist, and we all reminisced about the nightclub, the swinging Soho scene, Ronnie Scott's jazz club, Lenny Bruce's first gig in London and other matters of no particular importance. Although Mick Jagger turned out to be a narcissistic egomaniac, Watts and Wyman were open, friendly and masters of a certain kind of fast British working-class humor. I went along to rehearsals at an old air base in Newburgh, New York, and then to a performance in Baton Rouge, Louisiana. My acquaintance with Watts, and his generosity with his time, gave me almost completely free access to the whole elaborate process of launching a big tour. I got to know everybody—roadies, the cook, sound people, stage managers and all the rest. Through nothing more than good luck, I had more than enough material for the article. I had fun, too, but that couldn't go in. At least not all of it.

Twenty-five years later, the Stones piece is included in this book, slightly altered in chronology and its mention of jazz. The McQueen piece and dozens of other journalistic pieces have been left out. They seem dated now. A number of essays that were not written for magazines have been included.

A long time ago I wrote a memoir, *Stop-Time*, which ended when I was eighteen. A lot of people expected me to continue the story of my life, but I was determined not to write that kind of book again. *Stop-Time* stands alone, and I'm glad of that. I did not think of the book as the start of a career, I thought of it as a thing unto itself, and was astonished that I'd been able to make it. Decades later I wrote a novel, *Body & Soul,* as an homage both to music and to the traditional novels of the nineteenth and twentieth centuries, which I loved and which had awakened my imagination. But all along I was doing smaller things: stories, articles and essays that now seem—although this was never the intent—to extend the line of the eighteen-year-old boy, however faintly, into the present. But I hope the pieces collected here can be read for pleasure as is. It's the caravan that counts, after all, not the dog.

2001

Father

T HE TRUTH IS I hardly knew him, and have only a few
memories of him. He died in 1948, when I was twelve,
but he had been long gone by then, spending part of the
time in convalescent homes because of his manic depression
and heavy drinking, and the rest of the time, where? I don't
know. I was never told. For various reasons, my mother (who
may also not have known) put forward his illness to my sister
and myself as the sole cause of his absence. He couldn't be with
us because he was sick, which allowed us to maintain the illu-
sion that he wanted to be with us, and that only his sicknesses,
for which he was not responsible, prevented it from happening.

It's hard to know how much to believe of what little I've been
told about him. He grew up in Jacksonville, Florida, and his
mother sent him to school in velvet suits and lace collars, which
he deeply resented. His father died when he was a teenager, and
the language of the funeral service caused him to walk out of
the church, creating a scandal, and to reject Catholicism for-
ever. As a young man he fell in love with a local beauty, asked
for her hand in marriage while driving her somewhere in his
Cord Roadster, and threatened to crash through the guardrail
into the river when she refused. Such are the shreds and bits I
have of his early life—not much to build on. But when I was
sixteen, coming down from New York on my way to a job as a
movie usher in Fort Lauderdale, walking along a sidewalk in

downtown Jacksonville, a middle-aged woman rushed out from a bookstore and stopped me. "You must be Phil Conroy's son," she said. It turned out she had gone to school with him. It turned out that for a split second, glancing up through the bookstore window, she had gone back in time and was seeing Phil Conroy at sixteen once more. Something like pain was in her face. I was stunned. I sensed—no, I knew—that she had been in love with him. I stood there in place of my father. For a moment I *was* my father, and understood that he had once been sixteen, that he had once walked the streets of Jacksonville as I was walking them. I was stunned because I learned that at one time in his short life he had been able to elicit love—that some-one, somewhere along the line, this middle-aged woman for in-stance, had loved him. I doubted that my mother had, and I knew that I hadn't.

My mother came to this country from Denmark at nineteen, apparently determined to escape the petit-bourgeois repressive-ness (as she saw it) of her family. Her father sold beer for Tu-borg, and her mother kept house, forcing the maid, as she'd once told me in scornful tones, to "comb the fringes of the rugs." She had some training as a nurse, got a job in a fancy rest home, met my father, who was a patient there, married him, bore two children and was then more or less abandoned (except for the money his lawyers sent every month). She never spoke ill of him to me, nor do I think she felt any animosity toward him. Her few remarks in response to my childish queries about him, and most particularly her tone, seemed to suggest that the whole thing had been simply a sad misadventure and not very important, really. He was a "gentleman" who "dressed very well," had "intellectual and artistic interests," and who had come north to escape the influence of his "neurotic mother." When I asked what his work was, I was told that for a short time he had been a literary agent, but that he'd "always wanted to be a writer." Why he had not become a writer was never explained. "He tried" was all she'd say. He hadn't had to worry about money because he and his mother were "rich" and "owned real estate in Jacksonville." What I got from my mother was not that she loved him but that she respected him. She had married above herself, and there was enough of the bourgeois still in her to be impressed. She told me many times that he was a very smart man.

My direct experiences with him do not add up to much. A couple of short, terrifying episodes when he was flying on manic highs, behaving so clearly like a lunatic that, young as I was, I knew it wasn't really him, that he was a man quite literally possessed, taken over by demons.

The few times I saw him when he was relatively straight, he seemed to have no memory of the bad times, but remained kind, distant, perfunctory, oddly helpless, as if he didn't know what to say to me and was mildly embarrassed because of it. He would show up at our apartment—where I had lived what seemed to me my whole life, and where he had never lived— and take me down to the Automat for a treat. (The Automat, an elaborate coin-in-the-slot restaurant from the 1930s, served mostly working-class people, pensioners and kids from the tenements under the El on Third Avenue. The food was cheap and good.) Inevitably, he was dressed in a three-piece suit of the finest wool, silk tie at his throat, breast-pocket handkerchief, camel's hair overcoat, pigskin gloves, perhaps. He would pick a table near the front, sip his coffee and watch the street. I would eat apple pie à la mode and wait for him to say something that would change my life, but he never did. He'd walk me home and then disappear for another year or two.

Once he took me to Broadway (in the unheard-of luxury of a taxicab) to see a Danny Kaye movie. I was excited and full of anticipation, not only about the movie, but because I was to spend an entire afternoon with him. An extraordinary event without precedent in my memory. We had two seats on the aisle in the huge, crowded movie palace. As the curtains parted and the titles began to roll, my father sat gripping the armrests and I could smell his after-shave and hear his breathing. The titles took longer than usual, and I heard him involuntarily whisper "Christ" and knew instantly that all he wanted was to get out of there. How much panic, anger and despair were carried in that single word! I had caught a forbidden glimpse of the real man, and was almost sick with guilt and disappointment. (Writing this now, I remember that I also felt foolish, only eight or nine years old but feeling suckered by the whole bullshit idea of a nice afternoon with Dad. I felt used, I felt lied to and patronized, and I felt angry. I could of course express none of this. I could only hide it.)

Some years later he died of cancer. I visited him once at the hospital. He was wasted, half his face was paralyzed, and he spoke with a slur. I suppose he was on painkillers, but his mind seemed clear. We were alone for perhaps half an hour in what both of us must have sensed might be our last contact, and yet neither one of us could rise above the awkward, befuddled silences or the quick exchanges of banalities that had characterized our near-to-nonexistent relationship all the way through. I was much too nervous, and he was dying, and knew it. Freud says that the most important event in a man's life is the death of his father, but all I felt was relief, and a sense of guilt at not feeling anything more. The sad truth is it would probably have been better for us both had we never laid eyes on each other.

So, like countless other children in similar circumstances, I made up a father, created an image and admired it. He was rich and powerful and lived in a glittering world utterly unlike the sad, penny-pinching, shoddy-goods, poverty-driven world in which I lived. I might be eating Department of Agriculture surplus cheese from the welfare people, but that was an anomaly. Even after he was dead I assumed he had somehow arranged for me to be lifted out of the exasperating frustrations I felt at being poor. (He had, in fact, arranged nothing, but my fantasy survived for a long time, since his "neurotic mother," who outlived him by four years, left money in trust for my college education.)

I had his library, or at least that part of it that had somehow wound up in our apartment—six or seven hundred volumes, floor to ceiling in the living room. I started on the bottom shelf, read everything, and worked my way up, eventually climbing the shelves like a human fly for new stuff. Here was escape! Here were dreams to keep me enthralled while waiting for rescue. Dickens, whom to this day I love above all other writers, Tolstoy, Balzac, Conrad, Maupassant, Jane Austen, H. G. Wells, Shaw, Fenimore Cooper, Twain, Melville and many more. There were relatively modern writers—Hemingway, John O'Hara, MacKinlay Kantor (signed! "To Phil with thanks"), Raymond Chandler, Fitzgerald, Ferber and others. A treasure trove which I perused for years, reading, for the most part, over my head, glimpsing what I imagined to be part of my father's world. In my incredible tenacity I read Zola's *Nana* without knowing what a prostitute was. I read Faulkner. I read Henry James. I was obsessed, trying to decode everything so as to find my father in there somewhere, some trace of him.

Along the way, something else was going on. I believe that, despite my youth, I sensed that all these people were writing in the service of something. They were creating fictions in the attempt to get to some truths (which was what I was doing in my imagination), in a tacit acknowledgment that truth was complex and evanescent. And wasn't it just exactly that? My poor mother had lied to me about every even slightly awkward question—and there were plenty of them—I had ever asked. Her position was that truth was a private matter. (She knew I knew she was lying; indeed, between her convenient lies and my dreamy fantasies we were a fine pair.) But these writers took the attitude, in the very act of writing and publishing, that complexity notwithstanding, truth was public, and the search for it was public.

In my mind I skipped over the fact that my father had never published anything and thought of him as a writer, which would place him at least somewhere near the heroic men and women whose labors in the pursuit of truth I so much admired. I was perhaps fourteen or fifteen when I found a little black book, privately printed, a chapbook of prose written by my father, under some shelf paper in an unused drawer in the kitchen. Twenty pages of dense and difficult writing (which he must have composed in a single manic burst) that just about took the top of my head off. It described a man leaving some sort of hospital, picking up a package at a printer's, going into a city and finding a bookstore—the action buried deep under stream of consciousness, cascading images, indirect language and wild metaphor. It was weird stuff, no doubt amateurish and Joyce-haunted, but it fairly crackled with energy, like a jumble of power lines strewn across a highway in a hurricane. At the end of the narrative the man entered a bookstore, slipped a copy of a little black book onto the shelves, between the larger books by published authors, and left to find a bar. I instantly realized that he had done exactly that with copies of the book I held, sneaking into bookstores all over New York City. Shocked as I was by the fecklessness of it all, the childishness of trying to buy his way to an audience in an end run around the real world,

I was nevertheless an experienced reader, and the way the piece gradually revealed its own genesis, its own existence, and even how it might have come into the very hand of the reader—the way the whole thing folded back on itself—struck me as original and clever. He had clearly been crazy, but just as clearly he had been smart.

Well, who knows? I know what I became without my father, but what would I have become without my father's library? At an early age I recognized books as quasi-sacred objects with the power to give me many different kinds of pleasure as well as teach me something about other people and the world. Later, springing from reading, came writing. That wall of books was probably the single most powerful formative influence of my life—certainly far more powerful than the man who had collected them.

His life was short, painful and full of empty agitation. He began a thousand things and completed nothing. I suspect that in many ways he probably never grew up—his various illnesses and the shelter of his inheritance working together to keep him a boy right into his forties.

I have outlived him now by many, many years, and if he did not rescue me, I have had the good luck to have been given enough time to rescue myself. I have three sons, and in being their father I have to some extent become father to myself.

What is going on, after all, when I play a round of golf with my oldest two—young men now—or talk to them on the phone about the last Celtics game, about women, work or whatever else is on their minds? Am I not attempting to live up to the image of a father I formed long, long ago, and does this not suggest I am responding to my own needs as much as theirs? And are not all of us relatively lucky in this? I think we are, because we all, truly, need one another, and we can all, truly, count on one another. Phil Conroy is gone, but to some extent he is gone into us. Not such a bad deal from his point of view. Sometimes—to me—it seems almost miraculous.

1988

Scouts' Honor

IT WAS THE UNIFORM, of course. I have wanted very few things in my life as badly as, on the brink of my twelfth birthday, I wanted that uniform. The desire was akin to lust, and I literally counted the days. "Militarism," said my older, smarter sister, a mixture of scorn and sympathy in her voice, as if I had contracted some embarrassing illness. "Conformism." She may have been on to something with the latter idea. The power of the eleven-year-old's desire to join up, to become part of a large, strong entity (the Boy Scouts of *America!*), to have an official identity with a uniform to prove it, is doubtless the opposite side of the coin revealed later, in post-adolescence, when the desire is to rebel, to *épater* the fuckers at every possible opportunity.

Once I had the uniform, I had what I wanted. At meetings in the basement of a church on Third Avenue and Seventy-ninth Street in New York City, we were encouraged to better ourselves —to learn knots, yes, but also to start thinking about merit badges, about moving up to the top, to the distant and retroactively redemptive status of Eagle Scout. (The official handbook at the time told us, rather gently, not to masturbate. Cold hip baths were recommended.) Deeply and instinctively suspicious of any process aimed at self-betterment, I did my knots and my marching. I followed orders because I was a relatively poor kid and I wanted to go to camp. Boy Scout camp was cheap.

Once there, I tried lariat-making, wood-carving and various quasi-Indian crafts, but finally discovered the canoe. Perhaps it was the solitary nature of canoeing that attracted me, or the smoothness, the quietness of it. I developed skill to make up for my lack of strength, and became (my second summer at camp) a canoe instructor. A prize indeed, since the instructors were allowed to take the boats out whenever they wanted during the day and could get around the rules at night. I would slip out, hug the dark shore for a half mile or so and then drift out into the moonlight. Fine stuff, and better than any badge, it seemed to me.

The autumn of my last scout year, we spent the meetings in the church basement preparing for a "Scout-O-Rama" to be held in Madison Square Garden. We hustled tickets for many weeks, going door to door in our tenements and apartment houses. We practiced quick assembly of our "tepee" and our "camp," where we were to reenact various domestic tribal rituals as part of a "big tableau" to be presented in the Garden arena. Our responsibility (Post 104) was small but vital to the success of the enterprise. The buildup impressed all of us.

It was exciting, waiting at the edge of the arena, our scoutmaster's hand on the gate. At a signal, we were to go out there into the unbelievable brightness and construct our "camp" in ninety seconds flat. We rushed out, and I was so intent on my tasks—pounding two pegs into the dirt, lifting the "cooking pot" over the red cellophane "fire"—that I never looked up until I was finished. Through the haze I saw some elaborate ceremony going on, far away at the center of the arena, some totem-pole dancing and chanting business that I couldn't quite make out. Everywhere else, all around the perimeter and in toward the center, were hundreds and hundreds of boys doing *exactly what we were doing.* Same tepee, same red cellophane, same pot. The lights glared, the announcer's voice boomed over

Running the Table

WHEN I WAS fifteen and living in New York City, I was supposed to be going to Stuyvesant High School, and in fact I did actually show up three or four times a week, full of gloom, anger and adolescent narcissism. The world was a dark place for me in those days. I lived in a kind of tunnel of melancholy, constantly in trouble at home, in school and occasionally with the police (pitching pennies, sneaking into movies, jumping the turnstile in the subway, stealing paperback books—fairly serious stuff in that earlier, more innocent time). I was haunted by a sense of chaos, chaos within and chaos without. Which is perhaps why the orderliness of pool, the Euclidean cleanness of it, so appealed to me. The formality of pool struck me as soothing and reassuring, a sort of oasis of coolness, utterly rational and yet not without its elegant little mysteries. But I'm getting ahead of myself.

One day, meandering around Fourteenth Street, I stepped through the open doors on an impulse and mounted the long, broad stairway. Halfway up I heard the click of the balls. What a marvelous sound! Precise, sharp, crisp, and yet somehow mellow. There was an intimacy to the sound that thrilled me. At the top of the stairs I pushed through saloon-style swinging doors and entered a vast, hushed, dim hall. Rows of pool tables stretched away in every direction, almost all of them empty at this early hour, but here and there in the distance, a pool of light, figures in silhouette circling, bending, taking shots. Nearby, two old men were playing a game I would later learn to be billiards on a large table without pockets. The click of the three balls, two white, one red, was what I had heard on the stairs. The men played unhurriedly, pausing now and then with their cues held like walking sticks to stare down at the street below. Cigar smoke swirled in the air.

I had walked into Julian's, little knowing that it was one of the best-known pool halls on the East Coast. I was impressed by the stark functionality of the place—the absence of decoration of any kind. It seemed almost institutional in its atmosphere, right down to the large poster hung on the cashier's cage setting out the rules and regulations. No drinking, no eating, no sitting on the edges of the tables, no spitting except in the cuspidors, no massé shots, etc. Tables were 25 cents an hour. Cue sticks were to be found on racks against the walls. Balls available from the cashier as he clocked you in.

"How do you play?" I asked.

The cashier was bald and overweight. He wore, for some reason, a green eyeshade. "You from Stuyvesant?"

I nodded, and he grunted, reached down to some hidden shelf and gave me a small pamphlet, pushing it forward across the worn wooden counter. I scanned it quickly. Basic information about straight pool, eight ball, nine ball, billiards, snooker and a few other games. "Start with straight pool," he said. "Go over there and watch those guys on twenty-two for a while. Sit still, don't talk, and don't move around."

I did as I was told, sitting on a kind of mini-bleachers against the wall, my chin in my hands. The two men playing were in their twenties, an Abbott-and-Costello duo, thin Bud wearing a vest and smoking constantly, pudgy Lou moving delicately around the table, using the bridge now and then because of his short arms. They paid no attention to me and played with concentration, silent except for calling combinations.

"Six off the thirteen," Lou said.

Bud nodded. They only called combinations. All straight shots, no matter how difficult, were presumably obvious. After a while, with a few discreet glances at my pamphlet, I began to get the hang of it. All the balls, striped and solid, were fair game. You simply kept shooting until you missed, and then it was the other guy's turn. After each run, you moved some beads on a wire overhead with the tip of your cue, marking up the number of balls you'd sunk. So much for the rules. What was amazing was the shooting.

Object balls clipped so fine they moved sideways. Bank shots off the cushion into a pocket. Long combinations. Breakout shots in which a whole cluster of balls would explode in all directions while one from the middle would limp into a nearby pocket. And it didn't take long to realize that making a given shot was only part of what was going on. Controlling the position of the cue ball after the shot was equally important, so as to have a makable next shot. I could see that strategy was involved, although how they made the cue ball behave so differently in similar situations seemed nothing short of magical. Lou completed a run of nine or ten balls and reached fifty on the wire overhead. He had won, apparently.

"Double or nothing?"

Bud shook his head. Money changed hands. Lou put the balls in a tray, turned out the light over the table, and both men checked out at the cashier's. I sat for a while, thinking over what I had seen, reading the pamphlet again. I didn't have enough money to play that day, but I knew I was coming back.

· · ·

Sometime in the late sixties, as an adult, I went to the Botanic Garden in Brooklyn to visit the recently completed Zen rock garden. It was a meticulous re-creation of a rock garden in a Japanese monastery. No one else was there. I sat on a bench gazing at the spiral patterns in the sand, the black rocks set like volcanic islands in a white sea. Peace. Tranquility. As absurd as it may sound, I was reminded of my childhood experience of Julian's on a quiet afternoon—a sense of harmony, of a supremely indifferent material world entirely unaffected by one's perception of it.

For me, at fifteen, Julian's was a sort of retreat, a withdrawal from the world. I would shoot for hours at a time, racking up, breaking, shooting, racking up, breaking, shooting, in a solitary trance. Or I would surrender to the ritual of practice—setting up long shots over the length of the table again and again, trying to sink a shot with the same configuration ten times in a row, and then twenty, and then a more difficult configuration to a different pocket three times in a row, and then five, etc. I did not get bored with the repetition. Every time a ball went in the pocket I felt satisfaction. When I missed I simply ignored the fact, reset the shot and tried again. This went on for several weeks at a remote table in a far corner of the hall—table nineteen—which nobody else ever seemed to want. Once in a while I'd play with another kid, usually also from Stuyvesant, and split the time. After a couple of months I would sometimes play for the time—loser pays—against opponents who looked even weaker than myself. But mostly I played alone.

Late one afternoon, racking up on table nineteen for perhaps the tenth time, I noticed a man sitting in the gloom up against the wall. He was extremely thin, with a narrow face and a protruding brow. He wore a double-breasted suit and two-tone shoes, one leg dangling languidly over the other. He gave me an almost imperceptible nod. I chalked the tip of my cue, went to the head of the table and stroked a clean break. Aware that I was being watched, I studied the lie of the balls for a moment and proceeded to sink seven in a row, everything going according to plan, until I scratched. I pulled up the cue ball and the object ball, re-created the shot and scratched again.

"Why don't you use English?" he asked quietly.

I stared at the table. "What's English?"

A moment's pause. "Set it up again," he said. I did so.

"Aim, but don't hit. Pretend you're going to shoot." I made a bridge with my left hand, aimed at the object ball and held the tip of my stick right behind the center of the cue ball.

"All right. All lined up?"

"Yes," I said, almost flat on the table.

"Do not change the line. Are you aiming at the center of the cue ball?"

"Yes."

"Aim a quarter of an inch higher."

"You mean I should . . ." For some reason, what he was suggesting seemed almost sacrilegious.

"Yes, yes. Don't hit the cue ball in the center. Strike a quarter of an inch above. Now go ahead. Shoot."

I made my stroke, watched the object ball go in, and watched the cue ball take a different path after impact than it had before. It didn't scratch this time, but missed the pocket, bounced smartly off the cushion and rolled to a stop near the center of the table for an easy next shot.

"Hey. That's terrific!" I said.

"That's English." He unfolded his legs and stood up. He came over and took the pool cue from my hands. "If a person pays attention," he said, "a person can learn about ninety-five percent of what he needs to know in about ten minutes. Ten minutes for

the principles, then who knows how many years for the practice." His dark, deep-set eyes gave his face a vaguely ominous
cast. "You want to learn?"

"Absolutely," I said without hesitation. "Yes."

As it turned out, it took about half an hour. The man teaching me was called Smilin' Jack, after the comic-strip character
and presumably because of his glum demeanor. He was a Julian's regular, and it was my good luck to have caught him when
somebody had stood him up for what was to have been a
money game. I could sense that he enjoyed going through the
drill—articulate, methodical, explicating on cause and effect
with quiet relish, moving the balls around the table with no
wasted motion whatsoever, executing the demo shots with a
stroke as smooth as powdered silk—it was an elegant dance,
with commentary. A sort of offering to the gods of pool.

I cannot possibly recount here what I learned. Follow, draw,
left and right English and how they affect the movement of the
cue ball after impact. The object ball picking up opposite English from the cue ball. The effectiveness of different kinds of
English as a function of distance (between cue ball and object
ball) and of speed. Sliding the cue ball. Playing the diamond
points. Shooting a ball frozen on the cushion. How to read
combinations, and on and on. I paid very close attention and
jotted down what notes I could. (Overshoot bank shots to the
side pockets. Undershoot bank shots to the corner pockets.) At
the end of the half-hour my head ached. In addition to trying to
grasp the principles, I'd been trying to film the whole thing, to
superimpose an eidetic memory on the cells of my brain, so I
could retrieve what I'd seen at will. I was exhausted.

He handed me the stick, shot his cuffs and adjusted the front
of his jacket with a slight forward movement of his shoulders.
"That should keep you busy for a while." Then he walked away.

"Thanks," I called after him.

Without looking back, he raised his hand and gave a laconic little wave.

Practice, practice. Months of practice. It was a delicate business, English, affected by things like the relative roughness of the cue tip and its ability to hold chalk, or the condition of the felt, or infinitesimal degrees of table lean. But it worked. There was no doubt about it: when you got the feel of it, you greatly increased your power over the all-important position of the cue ball. There was a word for it, the "leave," as in "good shot, but a tough leave." And of course the more you could control the leave, the more deeply involved was the strategy—planning out how to sink twelve balls in a row rather than just five or six. Progress was slow, but it was tangible, and very, very satisfying. I began to beat people. I moved off table nineteen up toward the middle of the hall and began to beat almost everybody from Stuyvesant.

The most important hurdle for a straight-pool player involves being able to run into the second rack. You have to sink fourteen balls and leave the fifteenth ball and the cue ball positioned in such a way as to be able to sink the last ball (breaking open the new rack at the same time) and have a good enough leave to start all over again. I achieved this shortly before my sixteenth birthday, with a run of twenty-three.

The owners of Julian's recognized the accomplishment as a significant rite of passage and awarded certain privileges to those who had achieved it. During my last year of high school a cue of my own selection, with my name taped to the handle, was kept in a special rack behind the cashier's cage. No one else could use that cue stick. It was reserved, along with thirty or forty others for young players who had distinguished themselves.

I was a nonentity at school, but I could walk up to the cage at Julian's and the cashier would reach back for my stick and say, "Hey, Frank. How's it going?"

What a splendid place it was.

There's a lot to feel in pool, a physical aspect to the game, which means you have to play all the time to stay good. I've lost most of my chops (to borrow a word from jazz), but I still drop down to my local bar—the Foxhead—every now and then to play on the undersized table. It's a challenge arrangement. Put your name on the chalkboard, slip two quarters in the slot when it's your turn, and try to win.

There's a good deal more chance in eight ball, your basic bar game, than in straight pool, but it's fun. We've got some regulars. Jerry, a middle-aged man with a gorgeous stroke (a nationally ranked player in his youth), can beat anybody who walks into the place if he isn't furious at having to play doubles, at kids slopping beer onto the felt or some other infraction of civilized behavior. There's Doug, a graduate student who always looks as if he'd spent the previous night in a cardboard box in an alley and who hits every shot as hard as he can, leaving the question of where the cue ball is going to end up more or less to the gods, in the hope that they will thus tangibly express the favor in which they hold him. (He is a poet.) We have George, an engineer, who exhausts our patience by approaching each situation with extreme care, circling the table several times, leaning over to stare down at a cluster of balls in what appears to be a hypnotic trance, chalking up with the care of Vermeer at the easel and running through a complicated series of facial and physical tics before committing himself. There's Henry, who programs the jukebox to play "Brown Sugar" ten times in a row before he racks up. We've got students, working people, teachers, nurses (yes, women! Smilin' Jack would be scandalized) and barflies. We've got everybody at the Foxhead.

There are nights when I can hold the table for a couple of hours, but not very often. My touch is mostly gone, and bifocals make things difficult. But a bit of Julian's is still with me and, at the very least, I talk a good game.

1990

My Generation

I REMEMBER ASKING, as a very young child, what was in the newspapers when there wasn't a war going on. That was the Second World War, the war to eradicate evil from the face of the earth, the war in which all Americans believed. Victory gardens, V-mail, Gold Star Mothers, ration books and air-raid drills were the order of the day. People talked lustfully of three-inch-thick steaks, automobile tires and real butter. My father carried in his vest pocket his own personal sugar dispenser for coffee, and my mother could be reduced to tears by a run in her stockings. The rationing of food, the enemy without, common hardship, common purpose and the almost godlike presence of Franklin Delano Roosevelt served to unify the country as it had perhaps never been unified before. If the First World War, however bloody, had been a bit of a lark, the Second was clearly a war of survival. Americans did not expect to lose, yet they knew they'd have to fight like hell to win. The discovery of the death camps of central Europe resolved all questions as to what the war had been about. The forces of light against the forces of darkness, that was what we believed, and no American today can be untouched by that memory.

We hated the evil Germans and the treacherous Japs, scorned the weak Italians, loved the stalwart Russians, the plucky English and the wise Chinese. The double-fuselage P-38 was the fastest plane we knew about, the B-25 our image of power. It was, to use Fitzgerald's phrase, "bracing to be an American." Then came the atomic bomb, and it was no longer quite so bracing.

It goes without saying that the effects of the bomb on the American mind were profound. We who were children at the time, with our childlike sensitivity to mystery, magic and the unknown, with our social antennae fully extended to pull in all sorts of information, regardless of its usefulness (the ravenous hunger of children's minds, storing everything away undigested, stockpiling the recognizable, the unrecognizable and the ephemeral against a future time), were perhaps most deeply affected. We felt exhilaration at the indisputable proof that America was the strongest power on earth, apprehension because the power was mysterious, and most significantly we felt guilt, secret guilt that verged on the traitorous, guilt we could not possibly talk about. Our political apathy later, as college students in the Eisenhower years, seems to me to trace directly to our inability to reorganize those simple, propagandistic concepts of democracy and political morality which had been our wartime heritage, and which the bomb had rendered untenable.

The war ended, the United Nations was born at Dumbarton Oaks, and America moved into a new phase. We grew toward adolescence during the postwar boom, a period of expansion and prosperity unparalleled in the history of man, a time of busy optimism during which America seemed to concern itself solely with adult matters. The kids, and there were not many of us in those days, were more or less left out of things. We inhabited a shadow area within the culture—nothing was important about us except the fact that eventually we'd grow up. We were embarrassed at our minority and most of us kept quiet, attempting not to call attention to ourselves.

We were the last generation to grow up without television. The radio was our thing— *The Lone Ranger, The Green Hornet,*

Mr. and Mrs. North. When television arrived we greeted it in a state of tremendous excitement. Movies at home! Free! It was too good to be true. And of course it was. It disappointed, was oddly dull after the initial novelty had worn off, unsettlingly hypnogenetic, vaguely inducive of claustrophobia. TV was technically crude in those days, inferior in every way to the marvelously cathartic medium of films, so we kept on paying quarters to get into the children's sections of our neighborhood theaters. And we got a lot for our money. The programs changed every three or four days, with newsreel, cartoon, short, trailers and a double feature. I used to go to Loew's Orpheum, see the show and then sneak into the balcony to wait for vaudeville at eight o'clock. Movies were a way of life.

We became teenagers when to be a teenager was nothing, the lowest of the low. Our heroes were not of our own age group. For the most part they were athletes—Jackie Robinson, Joe DiMaggio, Sugar Ray Robinson. Our music was Dixieland jazz (a revival was going on at the time), pop music and, for some of us, bebop. (When I met my wife's aged grandmother years later, she turned to me, fixed me with her steel-blue New England eyes and said: "Ah, Mr. Conroy, I understand you are interested in music. Please tell me about bobeep.") At the age of fifteen I saw Charlie Parker on the stage of Carnegie Hall. Our clothing, manners and lifestyles were unoriginal—scaled-down versions of what we saw in the adults. We had no sense of group identity, perhaps not much less than the teenage generations that had preceded us, but unquestionably less than the generation that was to follow ten years later. We were mysteriously disenfranchised—the best-looking girls at high school would ignore the boys of their own age and prefer to go out with older men.

In college we were named. The Silent Generation. The Apathetic Generation. There was no doubt about it. The sleepy Eisenhower years. America in a trance, drifting leisurely through a long golf game while the clouds gathered. Among students it was hard to find a rebel, virtually impossible to find a Marxist, a mystic, a reformer or indeed anyone who felt very strongly about anything. When my roommate and I discovered secret fraternities in our college, a college which advertised itself to be fraternity-free, and exposed them in the newspaper, there was a bit of talk but not much more. Most students thought it was a ploy from the psychology department. One can imagine what would happen now.

We believed in civil rights but did nothing active about it. Picketing was unheard of, protest uncool. It was enough to send a few bucks to the NAACP, an organization we believed to be utterly safe, no more and perhaps even less militant than the Parent Teacher Association. We were not afraid of Negroes and so made no attempt, as the students do today, to identify ourselves with their power.

Our sexual mores were conservative in the extreme. It was the time of going steady. Fiercely monogamous, we frowned on playing the field and lived as if we were already married. Virginity in girls was not expected, but faithfulness most certainly was. Promiscuity, which we interpreted as going out with more than one person at a time, was a grievous sin. Our watchwords were discretion, privacy and propriety. Needless to say, we lived and breathed hypocrisy.

No one knew anything about drugs in those days. Marijuana, which was to sweep through all levels of American society during the next decade, was smoked, as far as I know, by only two students in my college of five hundred. Heroin and cocaine were thought to be very dangerous (as they doubtless are), and no one would have dreamed of experimenting with them. LSD, Methedrine and amyl nitrite were unknown. Mind expansion was not a meaningless term, however. We read Blake, Zen, science fiction, the Christian mystics and various studies on ESP and psychic phenomena. We blew our minds without drugs. I remember lying, at the age of nineteen, in the enclosed garden of the Bryn Mawr library, under the cherry tree, watching the stars for hour after hour, aware that light from unimaginable distances was collecting in my eye, getting high on the universe. College was a straight scene for us. We didn't come across pot until many years later.

Our literary heroes were more likely to be figures from the past than from our own time. Most of us felt closer to the six-teenth, eighteenth and nineteenth centuries than to the seven-teenth or the twentieth. James Joyce, whom rightly or wrongly we thought of as a nineteenth-century writer, the penultimate romantic, was a god. We took apart his difficult prose without the least sense of resentment, dissecting clues as eagerly as Talmudic scholars. *Portrait of the Artist* and *Ulysses* were books we knew well. The perplexities of *Finnegans Wake* were thought by us to be the inevitable result of the depth of Joyce's art rather than any failure of Joyce's mind. It would have been sacrilegious to suggest psychosis, and we scorned Stanislaus Joyce, James's younger brother, for having done so. Beckett was respected as much for having been Joyce's secretary as for his own writings.

Closer to our time, we admired Faulkner, Hemingway, Fitz-gerald, early Steinbeck, and hated Thomas Wolfe, Dos Passos, Sinclair Lewis and James T. Farrell. Among young writers we liked Mailer, Capote, Styron and Salinger (who turned out not to live up to our expectations). There was a flurry about Françoise Sagan, mainly because she was nineteen, but on the whole we recognized her as a creation of the advertising age. The Beats were just beginning. Kerouac et al. we greeted with a certain amount of suspicion, convinced that art was not that easy. Our standards were rather high, I think. The New Critics had filled us with an almost religious awe of language. We read F. R. Leavis, Edmund Wilson and T. S. Eliot, taking it all very seriously, worrying over every little point as if Truth and Beauty hung in the balance. The conservatism that colored so much of our experience did not evaporate when we dealt with literature. We defended literary art as if it were a castle under siege, in imminent danger of being destroyed by the vulgarians. In every college or university I knew anything about, the most hated course was Social Science, as much a result of the incredibly rotten prose of the texts as it was our lack of interest in things social. We winced at bad writing, all of us, even the mathematicians and physicists who were presumably more interested in symbols than in language. We were neat, very neat, and sloppiness of any kind irritated us.

Fitzgerald calls a generation that reaction against the fathers which seems to occur about three times a century. There is the possibility that time has collapsed since he wrote those words, that life has accelerated to the point where changeovers occur much more rapidly, but nevertheless it is clear that those of us born in the 1930s were not a generation in any self-conscious way. We had no leaders, no program, no sense of our own power, no culture exclusively our own. Rather than saying, as did the youth of the sixties, "Don't trust anyone over thirty," we would have been much more likely to say, "Don't trust anyone under thirty," or perhaps just, "Don't trust anyone." Imagining, for the moment, American society as a huge mind, the students who came after us can be thought of as presenting the unconscious—they were pure emotion, they acted first and figured it out later, they were the route through which revolutionary power is expressed—but most importantly they felt themselves to be a part of the social organism. We felt nothing remotely like that. We were much more suspicious of society, without faith in its ability to respond to our minority voice. We were filled with precocious cynicism. We were stoics in our youth.

Now, as we come into power, we are aware of the paucity of

our history. We have generation envy. How colorless were our
times! Fitzgerald's people believed in their world—it really
mattered who won the Princeton-Harvard game, it really meant
something to appear at the theater or the opera—and because
they believed in their world, they owned it. Until the Depression destroyed them, they must have had a marvelous time. Styron's people had the war, a real war, a long, elaborate educational event plunging them directly into life. They had to learn
to swim after they were in the water, and however sad their
time, it was not dull. The generation that followed rediscovered
faith. They are experimenters, revolutionaries and freethinkers,
possessed by their own creative force. They have their own
kinds of silliness, of course, but they believe they can change the
world. It is no accident that they follow us; they are in revolt
against the banality of those who immediately preceded them.
We will never be like them, nor do we want to be, but we stand
to gain from their example. Our strength lies in our fluency in
all languages now spoken in America, the old and the new. In
tremendously exciting times, we stand at the exact center of
American culture, ready for anything.

1983

The Basic Imperative

CONSIDER THE BOY. Any boy—the kid who packs bags at the supermarket after school, for instance. He has long been aware of the mysterious otherness of girls. But now he is drawn to a particular girl, the one with the brown hair who buys shampoo all the time. The boy is shy and risks considerable mortification in approaching her. He is astonished to find himself doing it. Surely she will ignore him, or worse yet, sense the fiend in him and turn away in disgust. It seems miraculous when she smiles.

So he is launched. Up to now it has been "girls," not a girl. To be sure, he has been in love many times—with movie stars, teachers, somebody's older sister—but always at a considerable distance. Buffeted between frank carnal hunger and the most rarefied romantic moonstruck agonies imaginable, he has till now really only loved an idea—the idea of the feminine, the other. Faced with a specific, individual girl, he must adjust.

The mating dance progresses. They meet, they hang out, go places together, laugh together, talk, explain themselves. Although his attention is total, more focused perhaps than ever before in his life, although he hangs on every word and can't take his eyes off her, his actual perception of her is dim. That is because he is looking at two things—the specific girl he has in front of him, whom he may or may not come to love, and the girlness embodied in her, which he has loved, and will love, all along.

And then one night, parked in some out-of-the-way place, in the darkness, loopy and trembling from hours of kissing, his hands warm from her flesh, his head filled with the delirious scent of her, he begins to realize that the impossible event may well be about to occur. She has agreed to move to the back seat. Once there, things progress rapidly. Ever since he turned off the ignition, the boy has been swept along by forces he can barely keep in check, the full power of which he has also sensed he must conceal from the girl, lest she be frightened away. He has pressed forward, but carefully, so as not to overwhelm her tacit right to control the tempo of events. Rather a gentle escalation, instinctively done, without guile, all the more remarkable considering that he is literally drunk with sensation and would have to think hard to remember whether it was Monday or Tuesday. He is in the midst of a storm, a great storm, and some kind of automatic pilot is guiding him. In the dark, chasing the girlness, he has almost forgotten the girl. He has been obsessed with getting her in the back seat, but by the time it happens, his perception of her has narrowed to the point where he misses the fact that she actually wants to get in the back seat. He thinks it has all been the storm. His storm. His blindness is almost complete.

When he enters her it is a revelation. Nothing has ever felt so right, so profoundly, self-evidently right. He is in alignment with powerful forces, and in some curious way his own reality seems reconfirmed, as if a fraction of the power had stayed with him, become a part of him.

Afterward, he is almost entirely absorbed by his own emotions. It seems a brand-new world, after all. But stirring now, faintly, as he watches the girl straighten her clothes, comb her hair, is the truly exotic idea that he might have something in common with her.

Consider the young man. By his mid-twenties, the dance has gotten more complicated. His male friends have gone off in a hundred different directions; there seem to be almost as many styles and attitudes toward women as there are individuals, and to make it more confusing, practically nobody talks about it. There are men who idealize women, men who fear them, men who use women, men who are used by them, men who pick women to impress their friends, men who pick their friends to impress their women, men who love them but don't like them, and on and on. The young man, as he watches all these guys he's known since high school, will notice an intensification of whatever character flaws were there to begin with, particularly in the presence of women. Even the most balanced individuals are taken over by various kinds of folly and self-delusion.

By now the young man realizes the women are different from one another. He no longer thinks that all you have to do is catch one to know everything. He has met women who don't seem to know any more about what it means to be a woman than he does. The matter is complex, to say the least. Each lover represents a facet of the greater feminine reality as he struggles to get some idea of the dimensions of that reality. By now he also knows there is no turning back. Alone, he is incomplete.

He takes the stairs three at a time, effortlessly, flying up to her apartment without a thought in his head. He feels light and alive. If he felt any more alive he would lose contact with the earth altogether. The door opens and she is there, vividly there, more real than real.

He sits on the couch. She disappears into the kitchen while

telling him a story about her cat. She keeps on talking while opening cupboards and delving into the refrigerator. Returning with drinks, she looks at him and her voice trails away. He hasn't moved, his eyes having held on the kitchen door until her reappearance. They simply look at each other, and in the silence there is an acknowledgment of what is going to happen.

He may feel a touch of that peculiar mixture of self-consciousness and expectation one feels in a concert hall moments before the music is to begin—a delicious, tense alertness, a sense of sliding inexorably through time toward that moment when the first chord will explode in the air. He says something inane, which breaks the spell, and she settles down beside him.

Their talk rambles, almost as if they were noting things to talk about at some indeterminate time in the future. He is animated by curiosity—how does this fantastically complicated creature see the world? She likes Talking Heads? How wonderful and mysterious that she should like Talking Heads! Of course, a lot of people like them, but that doesn't matter somehow. He imagines he can perceive her intent, her pure intent behind those words, as if synapses of her brain were firing directly into his own.

As they touch each other, in any case, they gradually stop talking. Gestures that began as simple reflex become more complicated. Each moves toward a kind of immersion in the other, and they are like skiers gliding down a gentle slope who feel themselves pulled faster as the slope steepens. At a certain point they simply give over. They surrender and let themselves fly.

Off come the clothes. He is entranced by the sight of her body. He drinks her in, as if he could somehow swallow her image whole with his eyes, as if he might somehow preserve and keep it. He places his hand on her bare hip, slides his palm up over the bone into the soft curve of her waist and feels something of what it must be like to touch a wild animal—a shock of delight. He lingers over her, and energy builds in him. He shakes with it, hums with it in pain and pleasure, until he can stand it no longer and sinks into her. Instantly, everything changes. He has passed over into another way of feeling. He holds her, and begins to move.

When a young man is in bed with a woman he desires, it is as if his entire life before that moment has been no more than preamble. He feels himself to be at the exact center of the universe. He is not going somewhere, he is there. He is not waiting for something to happen, it is happening. It seems too good to be true, a fantastically lucky accident, a cosmic windfall. He's afraid that if he thinks about it, he'll lose it, so he doesn't think.

Consider the man, and in this case the lucky man, who has met, loved and been loved by the right woman at the right time. He may marry this woman if he isn't married already, but probably not, because special conditions prevail in what I will call (without apology) the Grand Passion. It is an intense, almost transcendental experience, with its own trajectory, and it cannot last a long time. It is not love to make a marriage, it is love to make a breakthrough, which acts, as it turns out, to prepare the way for all other love to follow, under whatever conditions life dictates.

She is liable to be someone he has passionately admired from a distance, but with whom he never expected to be intimate. In secret he has projected over her every human virtue imaginable. He has been careful and correct in his dealings with her, as if she were of some rare, exotic species and might spook at any moment. Above all, he respects her. She is a person of character, with a unique soul whose temper and resonance he imagines he can feel in the air when she walks into a room. He respects her

—perhaps to an unreasonable degree—and may even be a little afraid of her.

They have seen each other off and on for many years at various social occasions. Since each is caught up in his own life, and the lives do not overlap in any significant way, they would not appear to have much in common. Thus they are taken by surprise, entering into an experience they hadn't planned for. It is *trouvé*, which lends it a certain purity and authority. A Grand Passion, by its very nature, is not arranged for, it simply happens.

Over weeks or months they become friends. He continues to control his desire to make love to her, feeling privileged to share her company. He responds instantly, however, when she surprises him with a sign. She wants him.

She is his goddess. We can laugh at him for that, but from his point of view it is absolutely true, and as he holds her body and breathes her breath, as her mouth warms his own, as he feels the quickness of her, the life in her, he knows he is at the source. He becomes aware of her yearning for him—he can feel it under his hands, feel it in her kisses—and he knows that she also senses the source. They are together in a new place of their own making, transforming themselves. It is electric. It is also a profound solace.

They press, they press. They want to sink into each other, bone into bone, head into head, hip into hip. They are angered by the stubbornness of their flesh, the lazy obduracy of their bodies. They bite, they pull, they strain, and nothing can stop them now.

When their union is complete it is as if, paradoxically, they have left their bodies. They sail, they ghost along incorporeal through space, aware of each other's spiritual company, alone together in some indescribable vastness.

He hears something. A dog barking outside, perhaps.

"The world starts up again," she says. "Like a switch." They lie together in each other's arms. They've come back.

If the boy is blinded by the force of this desire, and the young man does not think because he believes the whole thing to be lucky magic, the man begins to see and think. The Grand Passion goes on for months, perhaps years, and relatively simple ideas, which had before been only words, words he understood easily, become earned knowledge.

To begin with, he deals with the implications of the fact that the woman truly loves him. There was no reason for her to become involved with him, probably plenty of reasons for her not to. She is not *trying* to love him—because she is supposed to love him, or wants to love him, or imagines she loves him. Everything she does and says shows clearly that she *can't help* loving him. He did not create the situation, nor did he seduce her. She flat out loves him, for her own reasons, and that means that the engine that drives her is much the same as the engine that drives him. They are in it together, natural companions under a force that exists, as it were, above them.

The honesty prevailing between them allows him to learn swiftly. His imagination moves past the boundaries of his self-preoccupation. They both know their affair will end eventually, and she, no less than he, has no reason to do the sort of wishful thinking, editing, coloring and withholding that can mark the exchanges of two people beginning to construct or endeavoring to maintain an edifice expected to last a very long time through God knows what conditions. There is a lack of defensiveness, a lack of fearfulness, and she gives the best answers she can to any questions he asks. She will tell him about her body, her sexuality, her image of herself—indeed, anything he wants to know.

There are no secrets. From hundreds of bits, some large and some small, he begins to form a sharper picture both of her and of womankind. To some extent he feels like a visitor returning to a strange country, only this time with a guide who explains that he didn't quite get it before. This is not the mating dance, nor a game, however serious. This is straight. The greatest degree of honesty of which they are capable. He learns who she is, and on the way he learns about himself. He sees himself through her eyes and discovers what is important to her in him, and what is not.

Why does it take so long? One would think that given the amount of time and energy men devote to women, they would know them very well. But for most it is a long journey. A man's need for women distorts his perception of them. He projects his created images onto them, and they are often adept at allowing him to believe they really are those images. Further, men so often bring to bear hidden agendas of which they are genuinely unaware. They become involved with a woman in order to launch themselves into a new stage of life, or to live up to expectations, or to avoid loneliness, or a dozen other perfectly understandable reasons. Men are too fragile and too involved to see women clearly without a woman's help. There is more than one way for the scales to fall from a man's eyes, but the spontaneous, honest, generous, passionate love of a strong woman is perhaps the fastest.

1987

Leaving New York

I SUPPOSE the thought—unbidden and unwanted—first popped into my head sometime in the early sixties, as I came home from a night of playing jazz in the Village. My wife and I lived in Park West Village. Two and a half rooms on the fourteenth floor of 788 Columbus Avenue: a flat slab building, replicas of which I was to see many times on the outskirts of Moscow twenty-five years later. It was two or three in the morning as I walked up Amsterdam Avenue, cut across the side street and approached the building from the back. It was hot and unusually quiet—no sirens, none of the anonymous, mysterious screams from the street to which we had become accustomed.

Fifty yards from home something made me stop and look up. What was it? I'd walked from the Ninety-sixth Street subway stop dozens of times at roughly the same hour and never had I stopped. I looked at the towering wall of the building. Then, as if some cosmic sound engineer had turned a dial, I began to hear. The air conditioners. A hundred of them jutting out from seventeen stories of red brick. A continuous sigh, a humming, a muffled but deep windy sound, somehow ominous. I felt a mild shock at the realization that the sound had always been there, and yet it was only now that I heard it, as if it had to break through some filter in order to reach my brain and be processed.

Something like a revelation followed. All at once I became aware of other filters, other forces bearing on perception itself built so deeply into me as to escape notice. Hearing, but not hearing, the screams from the streets. Seeing, but not seeing, the ragged figure sleeping in a doorway. Reflexively averting my head to avoid the smells of piss and funk. Closing my ears against the roar of the subway. Automatically minimizing tactile contact with any public surface. And by extension backing off from processing the sudden ugliness—the fight outside the Irish bar, the psychotic spitting curses at someone not there, the beggars, the potential muggers, the depression on the grass patch to the left of the main entrance to 788 Columbus Avenue where a suicide from the sixteenth floor had landed, garbage spilling, rats dancing, traffic arguments—these uglinesses and others, a daily ambush of various uglinesses backed away from, not processed, effectively denied. I'd been born in New York City, and spent most of my life there, and all at once I realized what it had done to me. Tunnel vision is the metaphor. Of the whole sensorium, and eventually of the soul. It took no more than a minute, and the frightening thought emerged with unusual clarity: *this is no way to live.*

So, move to Brooklyn. Brooklyn Heights, to be precise, which at that time had not yet been "discovered." Another part of the city, and yet from the stunned disbelief of our friends in Manhattan, you might have thought it was another world. "Brooklyn! Why on earth would you want to do that?" For space, for a residential neighborhood, for non–thru streets, for trees, for quiet nights, for clean sidewalks—for a lot of reasons, the most important being our desire to have a child, and then another child, which would not have been possible for two responsible people living in an apartment on Columbus Avenue. (Although people had been doing it all around us, their children playing in the chain-linked fenced-in cement-and-steel playgrounds sprinkled here and there in odd corners of the complex.) For many years Brooklyn worked well for us. We congratulated ourselves on getting there early, while it was cheap, as more and more people came over from Manhattan, driving up real estate and thus taxes.

And if, after three thefts, it was no longer possible for our boys to have bikes, nor to go to the nearby park without a large group of pals alongside them, that was simply a price of city life. When parking spaces became harder and harder to find, it was an inconvenience. But when the City of New York became dependent on higher and higher parking fines and tow-away cash transactions, when the number of legal spaces was actually *reduced* in order to increase civic revenues, the situation turned sour. (Of course, only certain neighborhoods were targeted for these schemes: the middle-class neighborhoods, where the residents, thought to be "good citizens," would pay their fines by mail without the expensive business of having to chase them down.) It became impossible to own a car, and I had no illusions about who forced me to sell our beat-up station wagon. The City of New York forced me out, and many others, in the start of what was to be a protracted war, an economic war against its own citizens, which eventually drove out the middle classes almost completely.

My boys went to a private school in the neighborhood. (The public school—even for a parent like me, who had attended public schools right up to college—was unthinkable.) The boys would walk, usually with a few pals from the block who also attended St. Ann's. One of their classmates was late one morning and had to walk by himself. He was set upon by three kids from the neighborhood across the park, robbed, then taken to a deserted brownstone, where he was sodomized, hung out a

fourth-floor window by his heels, beaten, then released with instructions to go home, get money and return with it. He returned with the police.

Okay, one might say, things like this happen when you have
such an enormous density of population. It's a statistical matter
—so many criminal, sexually precocious juvenile sociopaths per
hundred thousand. Perhaps, although none of the St. Ann's parents put forward that view. But what I found even more ominous than the event was the fatalistic calmness with which sub-
sequent developments were received. The three young crimi-
nals were apprehended, released to the custody of their families
and told to show up in court. They did, and because of their
youth and the disinclination (in my view irresponsible) of the
victim's parents to have the boy testify to the details of the
sodomy, all three were forthwith released. Again I heard a voice.
This is no place to live.

But I hung on. The city was not without its delights. Music,
movies, my favorite bar, the excitement of meeting new people
after my first book came out. There was a kind of forward momentum I never questioned, but simply rode, night after night,
a continuous social stimulation to which I became addicted.
And the more my marriage weakened, the more desperately I
tore around town. Much deeply foolish behavior, and I blame
no one but myself for that. Years of hysteria.

After the divorce I subleased a one-room apartment in Manhattan. I had no job, unpredictable income as a pianist and freelance magazine writer, no savings and, at the age of thirty-five,
no plan. "Don't sink," my divorce lawyer told me. I didn't want
to sink. I could not allow myself to sink, and yet I didn't know
what to do. When the sublease expired and I looked around for
a place to stay, I realized I could not possibly afford the rents
that were being asked, no matter how my luck ran.

The Big Apple! It had been my city, but now I saw it as a vast machine which would only grind me down bit by bit, forcing me into escalating debt, the charity of friends or various other humiliating scenarios. God knows I had judged some of my fellow New York artists harshly enough—those who lived off women, or hustled the rich, or sold drugs or anything at all to keep from driving a cab—and I was not about to join their ranks. I had, after all, not only to look at my face in the mirror; I had to look into the faces of my children.

My story is so common as to be banal, but there it is. I'd been ambivalent about New York City, but also addicted to it. Personal catastrophe finally drove me out, cold turkey. My friends, vaguely threatened by such radical action, did everything they could to dissuade me. If Brooklyn had been another world, then leaving altogether was disappearing into another universe. It was, all agreed, unthinkable. An insane, self-destructive proposition.

In fact, as it turned out, it was how I saved myself. I did not sink, as I doubtless would have had I stayed. I built a new life a good deal less provincial than the old one.

1995

Small-Town America

I F AMERICA seems vast to us now, how much vaster it must have been in the imaginations of those living in it be-fore commercial jets, the interstate highway system, instantaneous satellite communications and the standardization of retail goods through franchising. American culture is not homogeneous today—not by a long shot, given the geographical concentration of the poor (on a scale undreamed of by previous generations), the new wave of immigration from Asia and Latin America (no homesteaders this time), and the bone-deep regional pride of so many of our citizens ("Missouri," says the license plate, "the Show-Me State"). Differences remain, but they no longer seem virtually infinite, as they once did. The mall in East Lexington, Massachusetts, is not much different from the one in Seven Sisters, Texas. It may be Pizza Huts, Midas mufflers and Wal-Marts that stitch this country together, threads running from Florida to Oregon, from New Orleans to Chicago, from Arizona to Maine, and the efficiency of the system is nothing to be sneezed at. (It's the envy of the world, in fact.)

But something has been lost, or if not lost, eroded: the stabilizing, civilizing, intimate communal experience of the small town. For a very long time it was the small towns that held the country together, that kept it from fragmenting as a result of its great centrifugal energies. If the first social unit was the family, then the second was the small town. Tens upon tens of thousands of them across the wide face of the land, as numerous as stars in the night sky, they provided the reference points for the moral sextant of the country. It was the towns, not the cities, that provided the underpinnings for the great American experiment.

What were the forces that gave rise to them? No doubt at first the economics of barter and trade played a large part. The image of the small town as the commercial and civic hub of an agricultural area perhaps fifty times the size of the town itself is familiar. The courthouse played a role as well, perhaps; certainly the general store did, along with the blacksmith, the barbershop, the pharmacy, the church, the school and so on. Representing sudden densities of population in the enormous, thinly settled or empty expanses of land, towns formed on the prairie, at the entrance to a mountain pass, at the junction of a river and a railroad, at the center of a fertile plateau or delta, at a convenient source of water power—indeed, almost everywhere the lay of the land provided the slightest encouragement. Economics conjoined with topography, and communities were born that knew exactly what they were about—to handle the harvest, refine the ore, mill the lumber, get the cattle to market, manufacture the item, give rest to the traveler, any of a host of missions responsible for the existence of the town in the first place. Towns flourished or withered according to how well the work got done, and people pulled together out of a sense of common interest.

Not everyone liked it, of course. When the towns got big enough and secure enough, the generally conformist mores began to be challenged. Pulling together sometimes meant thinking together, and some people felt confined. In the days of the American writer Sherwood Anderson—and that was not so long ago—or of Sinclair Lewis's *Main Street*, small towns were sometimes seen as ossified, intolerant, narrow-minded enclaves in which anyone the slightest bit different—the artist, the intellectual, the misfit, the genius—would eventually be crushed. Hence a kind of brain drain to the cities occurred. Very few of these exiles returned, because in those days, when the cities still worked, those who left the small towns actually did find the freedom they wanted without having to pay too high a price. (Today, one would have to be rich, insane or very young to move to someplace like New York, Los Angeles or Chicago. As many of the intelligentsia who can manage to leave those places are doing so, reversing historical trends.) But if it was a weakness of small towns that everybody knew everyone else, and everyone else's business, it was also a strength. There was a sense of communal responsibility, of taking care of one's own, that moved basic, hard-learned family values out into the larger framework of society. We should remember where the town meeting—that justly revered American invention—came from.

In a sense, small towns were a dramatization of people's connection to the land, a constant reminder of our rootedness in physical nature. From that, and from the tangible reality of the social dynamic in what amounted to an extended family, came a strong sense of identity, and more often than not, pride. It may be just a small town, but, by God, it's *our* small town, was what people felt.

From the vantage point of the end of the twentieth century, it may require a certain amount of imagination to move past the faintly patronizing imagery of a Norman Rockwell and get a handle on what it must have felt like to live in one of those towns. A ten-year-old boy, too old to have his hair cut at home any longer by his mother, walks into the Main Street barbershop to sit for the first time in the very seat his father has occupied once a month for as long as the boy can remember. Or a girl goes to Miss Hicks's first-grade class knowing that her mother also went to Miss Hicks's first-grade class. A man walks down the street and nods to virtually everyone he passes because he knows them, and they know him. A woman has coffee with the spinster sisters next door every afternoon at four for twenty-five years. Downtown, no one ever goes out of business —the soda fountain, the bakery, the five-and-ten, the movie theater, the hardware store, the bank, the hotel, all are institutions, somehow larger than life. The rhythms of existence are long, steady and even. The names on the war memorial in the town square are recognized by everyone who looks at them. Some who look bear the same names as those on the plaque. People came and went, were born and died, and the town endured.

Small towns were complex social organizations made up of rich and poor, Protestants and Catholics, smart and not-so-smart, ambitious and easygoing, moral and amoral, givers and takers, bullies and bullied—in other words, the whole infinite spectrum of human nature. As a function of intimacy, stresses between various groups and interests were a part of life, and could not be escaped as they might in the cities. As a crude example, consider a man who loses his temper after a fender-bender at an intersection and gets abusive with the other driver. In a small town he must be careful (and is indeed subconsciously trained to be careful) lest he make an enemy he will be running into for the rest of his life. In Chicago, of course, he could simply pop the other driver in the mouth and take off, never to see him again. At a higher level, people had to work responsibly to deal with each other in the attempt to reconcile forces and attitudes that might come up in deciding whether to build a new school, change the liquor laws, let the village idiot sleep in the park in the summer, put in a stoplight, change the zoning, declare a holiday, and on and on. These processes, and this care, exercised over generations, created an intangible moral center toward which citizens inevitably positioned themselves. Again, this must surely have strengthened their sense of individual identity.

Every healthy small town had that intangible *center,* which one is tempted to go so far as to call a soul. The center would arise not so much from unanimity or from conformism, but precisely because people were so different, and yet were persuaded by circumstance to find common ground in order to live and grow. People in small towns could not back off from their civic and social responsibilities because to do so could result in swift, powerful and potentially dangerous changes in their day-to-day lives, to say nothing of the lives of their children. The center may have begun with economics and topography, but it quickly grew to include aspects of the social, the moral, even the spiritual. It may be just a small town, but, by God, it's *our* small town. It's our life, in fact.

Now we witness the decline of the small town as an American institution. External forces have pulled at the edges to the point where the center cannot hold. A small island off the coast of Massachusetts, whose population had held at six thousand since the introduction of kerosene, is overwhelmed by the influx of money and people during the summer and finally ends up mostly owned by an investment corporation based on the mainland. The town square in Fairfield, Iowa, is architecturally intact but mostly deserted, the shops changing hands frequently to provide marginal services such as photocopying, video renting and the selling of science-fiction books, knickknacks, secondhand clothes and new-age crystals. Three quarters of a mile outside town are Wal-Mart, Sears, the supermarket, the franchise malls, and the gas stations, motels and Dunkin' Donuts to serve the interstate highway. The automobile demands its own kind of space and imposes its own rhythms. Tens of thousands of towns wither away because topography has changed and the economy has shifted. The common purpose has dissolved, and with it the idea of the intangible center. People turn inward, and nostalgia settles like a fog.

It is ironic that at precisely the moment America reassesses the importance of family values, the mechanism that most efficiently weaves them into society—the small town—is fast disappearing into history. For most of our children it will be a longer and more difficult jump into the world.

1993

The Mystery of Coincidence

SOMETHING LIKE twenty years ago I was living alone in a reconstructed barn on an island off the coast of Massachusetts. The building was partially furnished with stuff my ex-wife and I had brought up from New York City, where we'd lived when we'd still been married. Also a large Persian rug, china, silverware and various knickknacks I'd inherited from my mother, several hundred books and my old, beat-up grand piano. I had few friends on the island and spent most of my time wandering around the house, and the great expanse of moors surrounding it, in a condition of almost comically extreme self-pity, narcissism and bleakness, licking the wounds of divorce. I wanted nothing to do with the world or the people in it. At least that's what I told myself.

One day I was driving the garbage to the dump, and had turned out of the half mile of dirt road from my place onto the paved road leading to town and the dump beyond, when I saw a young woman walking up ahead. Blue jeans, quilted jacket, tartan scarf and short brown hair. She turned when she heard the car and raised her thumb in the classic hitching gesture as I went by. I had not intended to stop, but found myself doing so. Her face—which I had glimpsed only for an instant—seemed to radiate vitality, an almost shocking kind of aliveness that laser-beamed its way through the dirty windshield and my gloom-obsessed, three-quarters-shut-down consciousness. Some faint, barely functioning bell went off way, way back in my brain.

The garbage—two great plastic bags of it—was beside me on the front seat. (A gesture typical of me during that period. I was driving a station wagon and could easily have thrown them in back, but took perverse pleasure in having them right there next to me, like a couple of pals.) She got in and sat in the back seat.

"Hi," she said cheerfully.

I accelerated and glanced in the rearview mirror, tilting it. Yes indeed, I thought. Most particularly her eyes. Hope—like some glaciated mammoth slowly stirring in the heat of a miraculous arctic thaw—revived.

It was a small island. I got myself invited to dinner where I knew she (Maggie) would be present. I took her to the bars, the restaurants, the local boogie palace. She would drop by the barn in the afternoon on her way home from work doing the books for a rich old woman who lived across the harbor. We courted. I was thirty-six and she was twenty-three. She has told me since that the initial phase of the courting seemed to her to have gone on for a long time. It seemed quick to me. She lived on the opposite side of the island. When she moved into the barn, the tiny post office, unbidden, began to put her mail in my box.

I wonder if people are any longer able to come together as easily, perhaps even as thoughtlessly, as Maggie and I did in a time before AIDS, political correctness and general conservatism. Maybe they can. I certainly hope so. We simply took each other at face value, and in fact did not talk a great deal about the past. Maggie's family was vaguely Boston, but she had grown up in South America, Australia and other places where her recently deceased father had set up aluminum plants. Her mother and her two married brothers lived in the suburbs. I'd met my first wife in college and had two young sons (who would be joining us come summer, and in fact every summer for the next twenty years), my parents were both dead, and my childhood was described in my autobiography, which Maggie promptly read. I explained that for legal reasons all the names in the book except my own had been changed.

Neither one of us had any money, but we fell into a domestic routine shakily financed by freelance journalism and jobs I got as a jazz piano player. Maggie's vivacity was not limited to her face. She was quick, funny, energetic and optimistic, and she steadily coaxed me out of my self-absorption and back into the land of the living. Like most lovers, we lived very much in the moment.

And then one afternoon the telephone rang. Maggie got it in the kitchen and called upstairs. I picked up the extension, heard Maggie hang up and then had a conversation with my half-sister, who bears the rather exotic name of India and is a good deal younger than myself. I hadn't talked to her for perhaps six months, and we chatted about this and that. I hung up the phone and went downstairs.

"Who was that?" Maggie asked. "Did she say her name was India?"

"My half-sister. You know, the baby in the book. She's grown up now."

"There was a girl in my class at the Brearley whose name was India."

"You went to the Brearley?" I was stunned. "You didn't tell me that."

"Just for a little while. It was between São Paulo and Cali. We were in New York for a while."

It came to me that Maggie and India were the same age.

"That was her," I said. "She went to Brearley. It's the same person."

"You're kidding. That was your *sister* in my class? I had a fight with her once."

We laughed.

"I can't believe you went there," I said. "How old were you?"

"Oh, I don't know. Eight or nine."

"You know, my mother even taught sewing there, to cut the tuition."

Maggie suddenly got serious. "You don't mean Mrs. Trudeau?"

It was discombobulating. "You knew her? That was my mother. Her second husband's name was Trudeau."

Having met by accident on a small island thirty miles at sea in the off-season, having come from different cities, and given the differences in our ages, we had assumed that our pasts could have nothing in common. We sat pondering the coincidence that they did.

Maggie's eyes widened. "I just thought of something." She stood up. "Come upstairs for a second."

We went up to the bedroom, and she pointed to a silver cigar box on the bureau. "Didn't you say that was your mother's?"

I nodded. "She inherited it from her father and then it came to me."

"Wow."

I didn't understand what she was getting at. She picked up the silver box and we sat on the edge of the bed. "Why did I always keep it with me? In Cali, Sydney, Montreal, Boston and then here, I always took it along for some reason."

"What on earth are you talking about?"

"My project," she said. "My project with Mrs. Trudeau was to make a little needle case, a little flannel book with my initial embroidered on the front. We made it together." She opened the silver box. "Here it is."

Indeed, there it was, along with the other sewing paraphernalia she kept there. A tired-looking flannel rectangle with wide, childish stitches and the letter M.

"It was supposed to be for Mother's Day, but for some reason I kept it," she said. "It's been in here for months now. Isn't that strange? You could say the two objects wanted to come together." She looked up with a smile. "And they used us to do it."

We were silent for a time, contemplating the silver box and needle case. An eerie moment, but for some reason, oddly reassuring. The two objects seemed to exist in a state of profound calmness, a stillness which I noticed for the first time, and which suggested a sort of otherworldly peace. A peace safely beyond the possibility of disturbance.

"Hey, I know it's old-fashioned," Maggie whispered, "but you ought to write this up."

In the intervening years this story has become something of a family chestnut. When new friends ask how we met, we trot it out with a certain amount of delight, because it still seems mysterious to us. Every now and then people respond with a story of their own. The couple who discovered, after many years together, that the father of one and the mother of the other had been in love thirty-five years earlier. Two young American doctors meeting on an airplane on the way to a symposium in Salt Lake City subsequently find out that their respective maternal grandfathers lived across the street from each other in a small village in northern Sweden. The fellow who met his wife in St. Louis because she was driving a beige Dodge Dart he had sold to an engineering student in Boston years before. The young woman in California who eventually finds out that her husband's ex-wife had been her third-grade teacher in Sarasota. Coincidences like these jump out of our lives in high relief, and we never forget them. They seem to suggest that some great cosmic plan is being played out at a level beyond our comprehension. We don't really believe it, but we can't help entertaining it, if only for a moment.

1991

A New Father

W HEN I WORKED for the National Endowment for the Arts in Washington, I used to have coffee with a guy I'll call Saul. He was ten or fifteen years younger than me, and was one of the funniest, most charming people I'd met in years. His wife was a lawyer, and they had one child, a baby girl. "I don't know what to do," he said over an espresso one day. "My wife wants another baby."

"That's wonderful," I said. "Terrific."

"Yeah, well, of course. In one sense, sure." He took a sip. "But I don't know. It seems like we had Rachel fifteen minutes ago. I mean, what's the rush?"

"If you're going to have two kids," I said, "it seems to me the closer they are in age, the better." I went on to tell of my two sons by my first wife: born a year and a half apart, grown now and sharing an apartment in Boston. "They have very different styles, different personalities," I said, "which is probably why they're so close. All their lives they've gotten strength from each other. They went to different colleges, but when it was over they *chose* to go to Boston together. They *chose* to be roommates."

Saul smiled. "You're proud of them."

He was right. There had been much to be proud of when they were children, but this was a different kind of feeling, relating to what they had made of themselves as young men, how they had been able to build on their closeness and extend their mutual respect beyond the family nucleus, out into the world. I also felt, and perhaps Saul sensed it, a kind of relief—life is not without danger, after all, and now I knew they were looking out for one another, covering for one another.

I don't think Saul was surprised by my advice; in fact, I think it was what he wanted to hear. He knew my second wife and I had been trying to get pregnant for years. It was a familiar story: I'd met her when she was twenty-three, and now she was thirty-five and it was time. The biological clock was running. Pressure was on.

The thermometer. The charts. The monthly disappointment, year after year. Eventually we went to the medical people for all the tests—a fairly long and elaborate process for Maggie, who nevertheless checked out fine, and a quick one for me. (I still hold a warm spot in my heart for the doctor who leaned across his desk, holding my file in the air. "Spermwise," he said, "at your age, we're talking Clark Kent.")

It was a mystery. Everything normal, but no baby.

Not long after I left the job in Washington, I got a long-distance call from Saul. "Another girl," he said. "Seven pounds, ten ounces." We talked for a bit and I was warmed by his happiness. "I'm keeping my fingers crossed for you guys," he said.

It was a complicated situation. I'd been lucky with my children. Blessed, really, is not too strong a word for the gift of that deep love woven right into my existence. I was fifty years old, but I remembered and hankered after the intimate, fresh joys of new life in the house. I wanted a baby in my hands.

And here was Maggie, who had helped to bring up two children not her own. She'd been there, every summer for more than half their lives, dealing with the various stages. The screaming-yelling-and-running period. The water-fight period. The summer of night terrors. The years of socks—thousands of little socks gradually increasing in size to thousands of big socks

—along with strange shoes all over the house. The years of disappearing food: porterhouse steaks gone in an instant, gallons of milk dematerializing as if contained in trick bottles, the refrigerator seeming to empty itself in the dark the moment one had closed the door. The years of strange speech ("Eye-own-no," meaning "I don't know"). The years of boom boxes, visiting roommates and driving into town to the movies. The round-the-clock washer-dryer period. The one-hour three-times-a-day hot-shower period. The year of the visiting girlfriends. And much more. Maggie had come to love the boys, and had been tactful and sensitive in the tricky role of stepmother. She'd done the work, knew what she was getting into—or wanted to get into—and it was hard for us to accept that she couldn't now have a baby of her own.

Flitting around in the back of our minds was our awareness of what the doctors had called "options": fertility pills, *in vitro* procedures and the like. In fact we had read a great deal about these matters, but separately, mentioning nothing to each other, as if talking about them would somehow launch us into new and potentially dangerous territory.

But then one evening, after almost five years, the subject came up out of the blue. We found ourselves in agreement. We certainly respected those who adopted or who committed themselves to the long, expensive and sometimes heartbreaking route of *in vitro*, but those steps didn't feel right for us. The technological aspects of the medical procedures, in particular, seemed to us to be pushing nature in a way neither one of us, deep down, felt comfortable with. The "options" were out, and we decided to drop the whole matter and get on with our lives. "Maybe the best way to think of it," Maggie said flatly, "is that it's just our fate. So we accept it. We don't get a baby. There are worse things."

It was the saddest moment of our life together, and yet, in

our acceptance, I think we both felt a curious kind of relief. We would not do battle with nature, nor would we hope anymore, or wait anymore. We threw out the charts and the thermometer, and of course, in what appears to be a classic scenario, Maggie was pregnant in two months.

Despite the quantum leaps in the scientific knowledge about conception, it would be hard to find a doctor who hasn't seen dozens of couples to whom the same thing has happened, in one form or another, and to whom all that knowledge is, therefore, finally irrelevant. As the splendid and valuable work of charting the functions of every single gene in the human body goes forward, as molecular biology delves into the study of smaller and smaller entities, the relatively rudimentary and apparently easily observable process of conception is still not completely understood. Scientists can watch it all happen in a petri dish—can see the penetration of the egg by the sperm, note the instantaneous hardening of the shell of the egg, watch the realignment of cellular matter toward cell division—and indeed, so much is visible it might seem perverse to believe that anything more than the visible is worth thinking about. But the scientists themselves are the first to remind us that in conception, as in the relationship between the fertilized egg and the maternal organism that nurtures and protects it, more may be going on than meets the eye.

All of which seems to indicate that there is room for some quasi-philosophical speculation here, some guessing, if you will. Can it be that the state of mind of a given couple can directly affect their chances of conceiving? Some people want a child so desperately they become obsessed, and it doesn't do much good to tell them to relax. I've become convinced that for some people, as it was for us, a complete surrender to the prospect of a childless fate is a necessary precursor to pregnancy. It is as if nature insists on making it clear that the baby is a *gift*. And nature retains the upper hand all the way through, since there are strings on the gift. We do not own our children, we only have them and raise them; we share life with them, and a certain humility about the whole experience seems appropriate.

In the old days, back when my first children were born, few fathers took part in the delivery. We were given claps on the back and told to go out for a couple of beers, which had been all right with me. But this time my presence was requested. Maggie and I gazed at sonograms together, waited for the results of the amniocentesis together, did the breathing exercises and so forth, and somehow or other it became clear that I was expected to go the whole route. I'm very glad I did.

Maggie worked hard for many hours, and got close, but the umbilical cord was looped over the baby's shoulder in such a way as to pull it back after each contraction. When the fetal heart rate fell below the normal level—I watched it happen on the monitor—the doctors recommended a cesarean section. We zipped into the OR, Maggie was prepped, the incision was made, and Timothy was born in short order. "There goes the head!" Maggie said, although she could not see around the screen. I could, and she was right. "There's the shoulder! Oh, wow! He's out!" (We had asked not to be informed of the sex of the child after the amniocentesis, but the sonograms had more or less given it away.)

From the beginning, the atmosphere in the delivery room and the OR had been cheerful and mildly electric. I well knew the doctors and nurses did this every day, but they were excited, the whole team caught up in the unique power of the dazzling moment of birth. It was quiet as the baby's throat and nasal passages were cleared and he was checked over. "A beautiful boy,"

FRANK CONROY

someone said at last, "a perfect baby." Did everyone start talking
at once, or was it my imagination? A celebratory air prevailed.
Maggie laughed. I saw smiles everywhere, and the room seemed
purely filled with love. There is no other way to say it.

Tim's first birthday found us in Iowa City, where I was teaching. Saul and his wife sent a white sweater with a hood, beautifully made. The card said, "Time for another?"

"I'd be forty, or maybe more," Maggie said. "I don't think so."

"True enough."

"Isn't life weird?" she said.

And so one July morning we find ourselves together in the summer house in Massachusetts. Maggie chops vegetables at the
kitchen counter while I sit across from her, drinking a beer and
looking out the floor-to-ceiling window. All three sons are outside on the lawn.

Years ago I had installed a basketball hoop on the back wall
of the house, eight feet up rather than the regulation ten, and
the older boys are shooting, thunk, thunk, thunk. One boy is six
foot four, 190 pounds; one is six foot one, 185 pounds; and both
are fine athletes who play amateur-league basketball in Boston.
Timothy is only sixteen months old, two foot six, 23 pounds,
and has recently been trying to learn how to jump. (In the living
room, he places a piece of two-by-four on the rug, stands on it,
waves his arms around, bends his knees and sort of slips off.
He's got everything down except the actual jump.) Just now he
stands motionless, watching his half-brothers shoot. He is totally absorbed.

The older boys came to see him after he was born, and then
again at Christmas, and now they visit every summer weekend.
To them he must represent not only a new facet of their fraternal affection, but also a sort of rehearsal for the paternal roles
they will doubtless someday play. As it is, they already roll

around on the floor with him, swing him in the hammock, carry him on their shoulders and go into his neck for a quick nuzzle, exactly as I had done with them so many years ago.

The boys start running in for lay-ups now, and discover the ease with which they can slam-dunk into an eight-foot basket. Timothy waves his arms and makes some exuberant noises, his eyes never leaving the action. The boys pick up the pace, having found that they can do reverse dunks, left-handed dunks, backward dunks and, if they really push off from the ground, 360-degree two-hand slams. An amazing display, and Timothy is almost beside himself with excitement.

"My God!" I say. "Quick, look at Tim!"

Maggie leans forward over the counter. "He's jumping!"

Indeed he is. He flexes his knees while one of the boys runs in toward the basket, and then, in the instant the other one goes up, he flings his arms over his head, his feet come off the ground, and he is one inch airborne for a delirious instant.

All three are exhausted when they come in.

"Hey, Dad. He's coming along. Did you see him jump?"

For a split second, emotion stops my voice. I clear my throat. "Yes, I saw."

1989

Father Thoughts

A FRIEND OF MINE died recently. Bang, cardiac arrest at his desk. He didn't even spill his coffee. At his memorial service I listened to people sing his praises—how much he helped others in his work, how unassuming he was despite the political power he held. I agreed. Two or three times he was described as having been a good father, and I found myself wondering what they meant. I'd known the man for thirty years, and I knew he certainly wasn't a bad father—but a good father, a particularly good father? Was this real praise or simply an acknowledgment that he'd had three kids? What is a good father?

Not so long ago it meant being a good provider (usually the sole support for the family), being a fair but firm adjudicator in matters of child behavior ("You just wait till your father gets home"), tactfully staying out of Mom's way as she did the actual day-to-day work of raising the child and remaining emotionally accessible. So said society. Many fathers felt vaguely guilty, sensing there was more to it than that.

Today, the chances are a father's wife works, and that neither of them could provide sole support. He no longer has the option of staying out of Mom's way; to be considered a good father, he must pitch in at every opportunity. Despite the fact that Mom probably remains the "primary caregiver," to use the lingo, he must actively search out ways to do his full share. He must be creative in this. He must be generous emotionally to both wife and child. Not just accessible. Generous. It's a whole new story for Dad, except for the business of feeling vaguely guilty. This continues, since fatherly perfection, whatever that is, now seems even less likely to be achieved.

Making it even more confusing to define the "good dad" is the fact that the father's role, more than the mother's, is deeply affected by the passage of time, by the age of the child. We think of motherhood as constancy—continually adjusting as the child grows. Fathers begin by being out of it, no more than ghost mothers, really, until the baby starts to express curiosity about them. Who is this guy? What's he doing here? To the child, the mother is given, but the father has to earn his way in. He has to invent himself as Dad. He has to demonstrate his pertinence.

In his book *Identity: Youth and Crisis,* Erik Erikson reminds us that the world children live in is very different from our own, and that there is "a deep-seated superstition that [a] rational and practical man would lose his single-minded stamina if he ever turned back to meet the Medusa of childhood anxiety face to face again." It appears a man must actively overcome that superstition, must open both memory and imagination, in order to be fully useful as a father.

For example, years ago, when he was six, my youngest child had a short run of night terrors, a syndrome quite different from nightmares since the child is partially awake when he experiences them. The first time Tim experienced them, he ran into our dimly lit bedroom as if on fire, his arms flailing, legs twisting, eyes darting about. He came near me, trying to speak but unable to utter more than fragments, and I remembered instantly how terrifying that had been when I had night terrors at the same age—the realization that language could not carry any message about what was going on. Indescribable terror.

Tim wouldn't let me near him. "You don't have to say it," I said to him several times. "It happened to me when I was a kid. I know that you can't describe it, but I know what's happening."

He darted about jerkily, as if dancing barefoot on glowing embers. When he finally found his tongue he said, "I'm going to die."

"No, no. You're not going to die. It's already starting to go away. Believe me, I've been there."

At last Tim could look at me and hold his gaze in one place. I kept talking, moving closer to him, listening to his breathing.

"What is it?" he cried. "What is it?"

"Nobody knows," I told him. "Nobody knows what it is, but I know what it feels like."

Then he put his arms around my neck and held on tight as the terror waned, as the spiraling up ceased and the spiraling down began. He never knew how frightened I had been—from the first instant of his scream—not only for him, but for myself. Meeting the Medusa again. Really remembering, digging down, so I could try to help him.

One does what one does out of love rather than some notion of fatherly duty. Love is the engine, and what's interesting is that —unlike the mother, who often feels an immediate physical connection with her infant—the father has to come to love his child. The newborn is a tabula rasa for the dad, who may well be proud and anticipatory, but can't be said to love much more than the idea of the baby. Love arises as the father asks, Who is this child? What is he doing here? And watches attentively as an individual begins to emerge from the seven or eight pounds of potential.

Perhaps love between father and child starts in mutual curiosity, but wherever it comes from, it quickly grows, if all goes well, to a force as powerful as anything a man will ever experience. A true solace against loneliness, against the tyranny and emergency of self.

I am sixty-two years old, and my children are now thirty-five, thirty-three and eleven. I barely knew my own father, and if I had any role models for parenthood as I grew up, I suppose they came from books and from the movies, which even then I recognized as fantasy. My friends' dads—a doctor, a housepainter, an insurance salesman, a shoe store owner—seemed like nice guys, but were preoccupied with work and other adult matters. Nowhere in real life did I see anyone like Gregory Peck in *To Kill a Mockingbird* or Spencer Tracy in *Father of the Bride*—idealized dads, incapable of making a wrong move, who nevertheless suggested quite powerfully that strength, calmness, sensitivity and fairness were important qualities in a father.

So when my first two children were born, I had no useful role models. I was in my twenties and preoccupied with myself, my writing and my deep need to connect with the larger world. (If I'd had a father myself, I might not have felt so much the outsider, but who knows?) To a degree I now find astonishing, I more or less took my wife and children for granted. It never occurred to me that the enormous amount of time and energy I spent running around trying to discover the world and engage with it was in fact a kind of intoxicating mania in which I was hiding from my home life. With naive optimism I thought the domestic part would always be there and I could deal with it later.

My wife thought otherwise, and when the marriage broke up I had to move away from my boys, who were five and seven at the time. From that day on, I never took them for granted. I had joint custody, had them three months every summer and paid close attention to their needs. I was *paying attention,* words that I emphasize because of their importance. Paying attention is where everything starts. And it can involve more than simply listening to what the child says. My seven-year-old chose not to talk about the divorce, for instance, except for the single time when I told him it would happen, told him why, told him it wasn't anybody's fault and tried to deal with his questions (as well as his tears). After that discussion, he seemed to have no need to talk about it anymore, and I certainly didn't feel I should force the issue. But I maintained what you might call a heightened alertness. Was he adjusting, or simply keeping up a brave front?

A year after the divorce, my girlfriend and wife-to-be moved in, and I kept a close watch on the boys to see how they'd handle it. Would they resent her? Paying attention in these instances allayed my fears, but more important, what I learned while doing it increased my respect for the boys as individuals. It brought me closer to them. I believe the boys sensed a change in me and perhaps felt closer to me, and so the whole dynamic was launched. Paying attention became a habit no matter what was happening.

My third child, born many years later into a world much changed, was never taken for granted, not for an instant. It's true that by this point society encouraged more intimate participation from the father, more hands-on involvement, but it's also true that I had changed as well. Less interested in myself, I was much more immediately struck by the miracle of new life, more awestruck as I held my infant in my arms only seconds after his birth. I did not come to love Tim more than I came to love his brothers, but I was more aware of loving him. I was less frightened, it occurs to me now, of love itself.

· · ·

Assertions of the importance of fathers are easy to find in psychiatry and developmental psychology. What's harder to find is just what it is a father is supposed to do. For each man, it seems, it comes down to on-the-job training—such was the case for me, at least, and I can claim no special experience.

The fact that thoughtful people are unable to spell out fully and exactly what it is to be a good person does not stop them from trying to be good people. It is the same with trying to be a good father. One day at a time a man invents himself. Common sense, intuition, imagination, love and courage come into play as he attempts to embody the concept of a good father, which has existed up till then only as a vision in his mind and which he may or may not make real. Common sense will tell him, for instance, to do no harm to his child even in the name of doing good. Intuition will help him understand the child at a level deeper than language. Imagination will help him see the world as a child sees it. Love will make him pay attention. Courage will help him try to become the father that his child begins to show him is needed, and to face the fact that he will be needed in ways he has never been needed before.

Fatherhood is a constantly changing situation, one hour at a time, which in the end calls out everything in him there is to call out. Stretched over decades, it leaves no part of a man untouched. It goes without saying that pain, also, is involved. But that should surprise no one.

Yes, much changed in the twenty-four years between the birth of my first child and my last. Society shifted and concepts of fatherhood along with it. Economic realities have forced a re-examination of the fatherhood role, and that is a matter of importance. But the human experience, the deep discoveries inherent in fatherhood, the essence of paternity—these probably have not changed. At bottom the question of roles is secondary.

Who lies under the roles is primary. A man doesn't take on the role of father, he becomes a father. He grows into it.

Here is something worth considering. The child is completely dependent on the mother, so much so that it takes years to recognize her as an independent entity. The father, on the other hand, can be the first freely chosen loving friend, the first outsider, as it were, to receive the trust of the innocent child. The good father, then, is the man who can rise to that occasion, and stick with it.

1998

More Observations Now

ALL MY LIFE, from childhood through my sixties, I've spent more time reading than doing anything else. Sometimes simply for fun, sometimes to learn, sometimes as a solace against loneliness, sometimes to intoxicate my soul. I've read for more reasons than I can name, or possibly even know, but I'm quite sure that books have helped me stay sane, given me something to hang on to when my inner world — my mind, in fact — seemed near collapse. I don't mean books about mental health. I'm thinking more along the lines of whoever it was who said of Simenon's elegant Inspector Maigret series, "Who knows how many nervous breakdowns have been forestalled by immersion in these books?" Amen to that. (If it gets to the point where you cannot read, it's time to see the doctor.)

I can see now that books — the whole world of books — became my father, as odd as that might sound. I read, and read, and read, and then, very carefully, as a young man might speak up in response to his older and wiser father, I began to write. Writers are readers who stop reading for a bit to try an experiment. Sometimes the experiment works and sometimes it doesn't. It is perhaps the very unpredictability of the enterprise that forces people to try to take a closer look at what they are doing. Why is language so hard to control? How can you make a cogent structure when you don't know what's going to happen in the next paragraph? John Cheever told me, toward the end of his life, that he never knew, when he began a short story, what it was going to be or how it would end. He had to ferret everything out by feel as he wrote, moving forward in darkness. Not complete darkness, as I imagine it, but pretty damn near. Instinct, intuition, faith, selflessness are necessary. It is not an entirely rational process.

It seems strange that reading—usually such a calm, ordered, reassuring activity no matter what the subject—leads those who love it most into an almost opposite state of mind as they enter the stormy, confused, somewhat scary business of attempting to make a response. Maybe that's what reading is for, in the end. Maybe we wanted to be suckered in all along and just didn't know it.

2001

Think About It

WHEN I WAS sixteen I worked selling hot dogs at a stand in the Fourteenth Street subway station in New York City, one level above the trains and one below the street, where the crowds continually flowed back and forth. I worked with three Puerto Rican men who could not speak English. I had no Spanish, and although we understood each other well with regard to the tasks at hand, sensing and adjusting to one another's body movements in the confined space in which we operated, I felt isolated with no one to talk to. On my break I came out from behind the counter and passed the time with two old black men who ran a shoeshine stand in a dark corner of the corridor. It was a poor location, half hidden by columns, and they didn't have much business. I would sit with my back against the wall while they stood or moved around their ancient elevated stand, talking to each other or to me, but always staring into the distance as they did so.

As the weeks went by, I realized that they never looked at anything in their immediate vicinity—not at me or their stand or anybody who might come within ten or fifteen feet. They did not look at approaching customers once they were inside the perimeter. Save for the instant it took to discern the color of the shoes, they did not even look at what they were doing while they worked, but rubbed in polish, brushed and buffed by feel while looking over their shoulders into the distance, as if awaiting the arrival of an important person. Of course there wasn't all that much distance in the underground station, but their behavior was so focused and consistent they seemed somehow to transcend the physical. A powerful mood was created, and I came almost to believe that these men could see through walls, through girders and around corners to whatever hyperspace it was where whomever they were waiting and watching for would finally emerge. Their scattered talk was hip, elliptical, and hinted at mysteries beyond my white boy's ken, but it was the staring off, the long, steady staring off, that had me hypnotized. I soon left for a better job, with handshakes from both of them, without understanding what I had seen.

Perhaps ten years later, after playing jazz with black musicians in various Harlem clubs, hanging out uptown with a few young artists and intellectuals, I began to learn from them something of the varied and complex riffs and rituals embraced by different people to help themselves get through life in the ghetto. Fantasy of all kinds—from playful to dangerous—was in the very air of Harlem. It was the spice of uptown life.

Only then did I understand the two shoeshine men. They were trapped in a demeaning situation in a dark corner in an underground corridor of a filthy subway system. Their continuous staring off was a kind of statement, a kind of dance. Our bodies are here, went the statement, but our souls are receiving nourishment from distant sources only we can see. They were powerful magic dancers, sorcerers almost, and I can still feel the pressure of their spell.

The light bulb may appear over your head, is what I'm saying, but it may be a while before it actually goes on. Early in my attempts to learn jazz piano, I used to listen to recordings of a fine player named Red Garland, whose music I admired. I couldn't quite figure out what he was doing with his left hand, however; the chords eluded me. I went uptown to an obscure club where he was playing with his trio, caught him on his break and simply asked him. "Sixths," he said cheerfully. And then he went away.

I didn't know what to make of it. The basic jazz chord is the seventh, which comes in various configurations, but it is what it is. I was a self-taught pianist, pretty shaky on theory and harmony, and when he said sixths, I kept trying to fit the information into what I already knew, and it didn't fit. But it stuck in my mind — a tantalizing mystery.

A couple of years later, when I began playing with a bass player, I discovered more or less by accident that if the bass played the root and I played a sixth based on the fifth note of the scale, an interesting chord involving both instruments emerged. Ordinarily, I suppose I would have skipped over the matter and not paid much attention, but I remembered Garland's remark, and so I stopped and spent a week or two working out the voicings, and greatly strengthened my foundations as a player. I had remembered what I hadn't understood, you might say, until my life caught up with the information and the light bulb went on.

I remember another, more complicated example from my sophomore year at a small liberal-arts college outside Philadelphia. I seemed never to be able to get up in time for breakfast in the dining hall. I would get coffee and a doughnut in the Coop instead — a basement area with about a dozen tables where students could get something to eat at odd hours. Several mornings in a row I noticed a strange man sitting by himself with a cup of coffee. He was in his sixties, perhaps, and sat straight in his chair with very little extraneous movement. I guessed he was some sort of distinguished visitor to the college who had decided to put in some time at a student hangout. But no one ever sat with him. One morning I approached his table and asked if I could join him.

"Certainly," he said. "Please do." He had perhaps the clearest eyes I had ever seen, like blue ice, and to be held in their steady gaze was not, at first, an entirely comfortable experience. His eyes gave nothing away about himself while at the same time creating in me the eerie impression that he was looking directly into my soul. He asked a few quick questions, as if to put me at my ease, and we fell into conversation. He was William O. Douglas of the Supreme Court, and when he saw how startled I was, he said, "Call me Bill. Now tell me what you're studying and why you get up so late in the morning." Thus began a series of talks that stretched over many weeks. The fact that I was an ignorant sophomore with literary pretensions who knew nothing about the law didn't seem to bother him. We talked about everything from Shakespeare to the possibility of life on other planets. One day I mentioned that I was going to have dinner with Judge Learned Hand. I explained that Hand was my girlfriend's grandfather. Douglas nodded, but I could tell he was surprised at the coincidence of my knowing the senior judge of the most important court in the country save the Supreme Court itself. After fifty years on the bench, Judge Hand had become a famous man, both in and out of legal circles—a living legend, to his own dismay. "Tell him hello and give him my best regards," Douglas said.

Learned Hand, in his eighties, was a short, barrel-chested man with a large square head, huge, thick, bristling eyebrows and soft brown eyes. He radiated energy and would sometimes bark out remarks or questions in the living room as if he were in court. His humor was sharp, but often leavened with a touch of self-mockery. When something caught his funny bone he would burst out with explosive laughter—the laughter of a man who enjoyed laughing. He had a large repertoire of dramatic expressions involving the use of his eyebrows—very useful, he told me conspiratorially, when looking down on things from behind the bench. (The court stenographer could not record the movement of his eyebrows.) When I told him I'd been talking to William O. Douglas, they first shot up in exaggerated surprise and then lowered and moved forward in a glower.

"*Justice* William O. Douglas, young man," he admonished. "Justice Douglas, if you please." About the Supreme Court in general, Hand insisted on a tone of profound respect. Little did I know that in private correspondence he had referred to the Court as "The Blessed Saints, Cherubim and Seraphim," "The Jolly Boys," "The Nine Tin Jesuses," "The Nine Blameless Ethiopians" and, my particular favorite, "The Nine Blessed Chalices of the Sacred Effluvium."

Hand was badly stooped and had a lot of pain in his lower back. Martinis helped, but his strict Yankee wife approved of only one before dinner. It was my job to make the second and somehow slip it to him. If the pain was especially acute, he would get out of his chair and lie flat on the rug, still talking, and finish his point without missing a beat. He flattered me by asking for my impression of Justice Douglas, instructed me to convey his warmest regards and began talking about the Dennis case, which he described as a particularly tricky and difficult case involving the prosecution of eleven leaders of the Communist party. He had just started in on the First Amendment and free speech when we were called in to dinner.

William O. Douglas loved the outdoors, and we fell into the habit of having coffee in the Coop and then strolling under the trees down to the duck pond. About the Dennis case, he said something to this effect: "Eleven Communists arrested by the government. Up to no good, said the government; dangerous people, violent overthrow, etc. First Amendment, said the defense; freedom of speech, etc." Douglas stopped walking. "Clear and present danger."

"What?" I asked. He often talked in a telegraphic manner, and one was expected to keep up with him. It was sometimes like listening to a man thinking out loud.

"Clear and present danger," he said. "That was the issue. Did they constitute a clear and present danger? I don't think so. I think everybody took the language pretty far in Dennis." He began walking, striding along quickly. Again, one was expected to keep up with him. "The FBI was all over them. Phones tapped, constant surveillance. How could it be clear and present danger with the FBI watching every move they made? That's a ginkgo," he said suddenly, pointing at a tree. "A beauty. You don't see those every day. Ask Hand about clear and present danger."

I was in fact reluctant to do so. Douglas's argument seemed to me to be crushing—the last word, really—and I didn't want to embarrass Judge Hand. But back in the living room, on the second martini, the old man asked about Douglas. I sort of scratched my nose and recapitulated the conversation by the ginkgo tree.

"What?" Hand shouted. "Speak up, sir, for heaven's sake."

"He said the FBI was watching them all the time, so there couldn't be a clear and present danger," I blurted out, blushing as I said it.

A terrible silence filled the room. Hand's eyebrows writhed on his face like two huge caterpillars. He leaned forward in the wing chair, his face finally settling into a grim expression. "I am astonished," he said softly, his eyes holding mine, "at Justice Douglas's newfound faith in the Federal Bureau of Investigation." His big granite head moved even closer to mine, until I could smell the martini. "I had understood him to consider it a politically corrupt, incompetent organization, directed by a power-crazed lunatic." I realized I had been holding my breath throughout all of this, and as I relaxed, I saw the faintest trace of a smile cross Hand's face. Things are sometimes more complicated than they first appear, his smile seemed to say. The old man leaned back. "The proximity of the danger is something to think about. Ask him about that. See what he says."

I chewed the matter over as I returned to campus. Hand had quoted some of Douglas's language about the FBI from other sources which seemed to bear out his point. I thought about the words "clear and present danger," and the fact that if you looked at them closely, they might not be as simple as they had first appeared. What degree of danger? Did the word "present" allude to the proximity of the danger, or just the fact that the danger was there at all—that it wasn't an anticipated danger? Were there other hidden factors these great men were weighing of which I was unaware?

But Douglas was gone, back to Washington. (The writer in me is tempted to create a scene here—to invent one for dramatic purposes—but of course I can't do that.) My brief time as a messenger boy was over, and I felt a certain frustration, as if, with a few more exchanges, the matter of *Dennis et al.* v. *United States* might have been resolved to my satisfaction. They'd left me high and dry. But it is precisely because the matter was left unresolved that I have thought about it, off and on, all these years. "The Constitution," Hand used to say to me flatly, "is a piece of paper. The Bill of Rights is a piece of paper." It was many years before I understood what he meant. Documents alone do not keep democracy alive, nor maintain the rule of law. There is no particular safety in them. Living men and women, generation after generation, must continually remake democracy and the law, and that involves an ongoing state of tension between the past and the present which will never be completely resolved.

Education doesn't end until life ends, because you never know when you're going to understand something you hadn't understood before. For me, the magic dance of the shoeshine men was the sort of experience in which understanding came with a click, a resolving kind of click. The same with the experience at the piano. What happened with Justice Douglas and Judge Hand was different, and makes the point that understanding does not always mean resolution. Indeed, in our intellectual lives, our creative lives, it is perhaps those problems that will never resolve that rightly claim the lion's share of our energies. The physical body exists in a constant state of tension as it maintains homeostasis, and so too does the active mind embrace the tension of never being certain, never being absolutely sure, never being finished as it engages the world. That is our special fate, our inexpressibly valuable condition.

1988

My Teacher

I T WAS FOUR A.M. in Iowa City. I woke in time to stretch out my arm, push the button and prevent the alarm from sounding. My wife, and in the next room my young son, slept on. I got dressed in the dark—shirt and tie, my best suit, black shoes, all of it laid out the previous evening—and tiptoed downstairs to the kitchen for coffee. Staring out at the blackness on the other side of the window, I felt oddly self-conscious. Should I go? No one had invited me. The only reason I knew about it was because of a call from my old college roommate, who knew I'd want to know. Certainly this was not a social duty. I could wait a few hours, call my old roommate and tell him not to bother picking me up, fabricate some inescapable conflict, change my clothes and stick to my daily routine. Forgo the melodrama, said a voice in my head. He was your first reader and your first editor, said another voice, the first person ever to talk to you seriously about writing, ever to take you seriously. So I went out the door, drove to the airport near Cedar Rapids, flew to St. Louis, waited an hour, flew to Philadelphia, got picked up and made it to the Quaker meetinghouse on time. The building had not changed in thirty-five years, but a lot of other things, as I was soon to hear, had changed drastically.

In 1954 I was a skinny, long-haired, pigeon-toed, overly intense eighteen-year-old kid with a face full of acne. I'd managed to get into a very good, small Quaker college (despite a miserable showing in high school), and I wanted desperately to be a writer. Since the age of ten or eleven, books had been more real to me than the actual world, and now I wanted to go even deeper. I wanted to write myself.

My teacher for freshman English was a man I will call Professor Cipher, whom I first met at an informal student-faculty mixer under a striped tent behind the library a few days before the start of classes. Cipher looked to be in his mid-thirties and was, in fact, moderately ugly. A Swinburne chin; fleshy, moist lips; coarse, curly black hair; thick glasses in heavy black frames; and stained teeth. We stood on the impossibly green grass and chatted about I can't remember what. But I do remember the speed and agility of his mind, his intensity and an air of mild cynicism, which for some reason I thought was terrific. (Professor Cipher had graduated at the top of his class at Harvard, where he had also acquired a certain style, a certain intellectual dandyism, which he could turn on and off at will.)

Freshman English at my college was a demanding course: full seminar twice a week, a syllabus of perhaps thirty books, a written paper every week and a tutorial to discuss that paper in the professor's office, head to head, for the better part of an hour. (Quite a workload for the teacher, but I never thought about it back then.) Professor Cipher had *published a novel,* so I thought to capture his attention by handing in a dramatization of our meeting under the striped tent—third-person, past-tense—in which I added to my own dialogue (that is, "the student") a good deal more intellectual dandyism than had been expressed in the actual event.

Professor Cipher's office was a small room with a window, a desk and a couple of folding chairs. Books covered all four walls and most of the floor. There were no shelves, simply stacks of books four or five feet high leaning precariously against the walls, mounds of books in corners, books strewn across the floor, occasional open volumes whose pages would flip at a breeze through the open window. I handled my own books with reverence and stored them neatly; Professor Cipher seemed to use a shovel. But the shock left almost instantly, and suddenly the disorder seemed thrilling—some kind of rejection of materialism, perhaps, or simply the urge literally to swim in books, or a vaguely aristocratic disdain for order. Whatever it was, I thought, it was probably very Harvard, very Oxford and Cambridge, and therefore magically wonderful.

"Ah, yes. Mr. Conroy," he said, shuffling through the papers on his desk. "Come around and sit here where you can see." He found my four-page double-spaced paper. I saw with alarm that the first page was covered with red markings. "Pay attention," he said. "I'll walk you through this time, but in the future it'll be up to you to figure out what I mean." He gave a slightly evil chuckle. Then, tapping the pages every now and then to indicate one of his red marks, he began talking very rapidly. "Much is self-explanatory. 'Awk' is 'awkward,' usually a question of rhythm, usage, grammar or overwriting. 'Cli' is 'cliché.' 'Rep' is 'repetition,' something you've already said, a device you've already used or a stylistic tic. 'Unc' is 'unclear,' which means either I don't understand what you're saying or you're saying something that can be understood in more than one way. I mean the *literal* meaning. You understand?"

"I think so," I said, attempting to conceal my excitement. I had always written by instinct, and the idea that he was taking my writing seriously enough to do line-by-line editing made me tremble. As well, his implicit suggestion that there were some loose rules I might apply—that, indeed, a certain amount of thought and caution was appropriate while writing—struck me as potentially valuable, even radical, since these things might reduce my dependency on instinct. I truly loved to write, but deep down I was unsettled by the fact that I didn't really know what I was doing.

"Indent your paragraphs," he said, tapping the page. "Seven spaces. When you switch from one character speaking to the other character, you should, in most cases, make a new paragraph. It helps in attribution, so you can avoid this sort of thing."

"What sort of thing?"

"Down here. Look how you're falling all over yourself to let us know who's talking. It's clumsy."

Indeed, now that he'd pointed it out, it seemed exceedingly clumsy. "Okay. Yes. I see what you mean."

"Why do you put all these dots at the end of these lines of dialogue? You do it a lot."

"Uh, I guess, well, you know, the way people trail off sometimes, or leave words hanging in the air."

He gave a deep sigh. "Would you reinvent the wheel? Why not simply learn the conventions as they have been handed down to us? Dots at the end of a line of dialogue mean the speaker has been *interrupted.* That's what they *mean,* and you can't use them as you use them here. Think of the *reader,* sir." He removed his glasses and stared at me with almost theatrical intensity.

Then he bent over and rummaged through some books on the floor. Finally, he straightened up and handed me a beat-up copy of *The Chicago Manual of Style.* "Read this," he said. "Get Strunk and White and read that."

"Who, sir?"

"Strunk and White. *The Elements of Style.* We used to call it 'the *little* book.'" Again the odd chuckle.

"Yes, sir."

He returned to my manuscript. "When you see my red

marks, you'll usually be able to go to one or the other of those books for more information."

"What about the blue marks?" I asked.

"An indication that I liked it, whatever it is." He turned a page. "Here, for instance, the way they drink punch from those little paper cups. A good detail, those cups. They capture the triviality of it all." He turned another page. "Your similes are occasionally fresh. Your details sometimes well chosen."

If I blushed, Professor Cipher did not seem to notice. I had expected him to say at least something about the fact that I'd written about *us*, about our first meeting, about reality (as I naively thought), but that was clearly not in the cards. His approach to the manuscript was completely technical.

"Give me some more next week," he said. "Something different."

"What about the *Gatsby* paper?"

"Yes, yes. Do the *Gatsby* paper. But give me some dramatized narrative as well."

"You mean a story?"

"A sketch, a story." He waved his hand in the air, shooing me out as he looked for something in a drawer, mumbling to himself as if I weren't there.

And so it began. When I got my stories and sketches back, I would immediately go to the blue markings, savoring his brief marginalia ("Good" or "Very good"), trying to winkle out why he'd liked whatever he'd marked. I studied his red markings even more carefully, anticipating the awks, uncs, reps and other simple errors he might mark, and correcting them in rewrite, so that his red markings tended to get longer and sometimes vaguer ("Not sure about this" or "A barbarism, sir. Watch your usage" or "Despite the control of language, this moment is melodramatic, and sinks the scene"). In tutorial he spoke very little about grand aesthetic or philosophical matters; he stuck to the text, however juvenile or banal it might have been, and pressed forward with writing strategies and the implications of same ("Should this be in first person? Have you considered third person omniscient for this?") and continual suggestions as to what I should read. He was the first person I'd ever met who thought it was not only normal but in fact a *given* that I would read one or two books a day. Since I'd been doing it since childhood (in a haphazard way), I was reassured.

I did not particularly enjoy his novel, even as I recognized that it was well written. It lacked heat for me somehow, but in my eagerness to preserve him as hero, authority, editor, sophisticate and all the other things that I needed him to be, I assumed I was simply too young for his book. (In fact, he had given up on fiction and never written another novel. His was perfunctory—a word, by the way, I learned from him.)

As the term progressed, he allowed me to concentrate entirely on fiction, and I knew this was a unique arrangement. He accepted me as a writer and automatically gave an A– to everything I turned in, even though we both knew the quality varied. The tacit message was that I was special and that the work we were doing was somehow above grades, above ordinary academic pursuits. In seminar I was exempt from the whiplash sarcasm with which he terrorized my classmates—half of them, as he well knew, bound for medical school. If I screwed up, the worst I could expect would be a classical allusion to flying too close to the sun. Others would not be let off so lightly. If he sensed any sort of intellectual dishonesty, he would work a kid over with sadistic glee. He was very, very good at that.

I relished every moment I spent with the man, especially tutorial. I worked hard to be worthy of his faith and rapidly gained control of my language. ("You are a racehorse," he once said to me, "among elephants." I glowed for weeks.) He was no doubt "projecting" (as the psychoanalysts used to say) onto me. His youthful artistic ambitions, perhaps. Much more, I was "projecting" onto him, seeing him as something close to a god on earth. I was devastated when, toward the end of my freshman year, he casually mentioned that he was going to Japan for two years for some special project. I can see now that the two-year separation only exacerbated my projection or transference or whatever it was (love?), to the degree that it actually made it harder to work with him when he finally did return.

That last year we did some good work. I sold my first story and began getting letters of encouragement from people like John Crowe Ransom and Elizabeth Bowen, thus legitimizing—to the college and to ourselves—the original special arrangement. But between the two of us there was a slightly dampening self-consciousness. A sense of caution. On his part, the faculty had warned him that I'd talked about him all during his absence, making a father figure out of him. For me, there were doubtless subterranean fears that he couldn't live up to the image I had created of him. Nevertheless, as I've said, we got a lot of work done, and when we said goodbye after graduation, I think we both felt proud. "You're going to be a writer" were his final words. "Better find yourself a rich wife." And then—a breathtakingly daring and uncharacteristic thing for him to do —he gave me a fast little hug.

I married a moderately rich girl, and with $300 a month (eroding the capital of a small inheritance from my grandmother) I was able to avoid having a job. I spent my days reading and writing. Four years on my first book, a novel that was a good deal worse than perfunctory—some nice writing here and there, but flat-out dead, like a stillborn baby. I'd had profound doubts about it all along, finishing it more from a sense of tenacity than anything else. Six months of confusion and soul-searching followed. My God, how desperately I wanted to be a writer. Then I began a new book—an autobiography. Four and a half years later I had *Stop-Time,* which sold only seven thousand copies in hardback but made a big splash critically and gave me an entrée to literary life in New York.

Professor Cipher read the book, admired it and arranged for me to come back to the college to address the students. I was grateful for the opportunity to express my debt to him formally and publicly. He was pleased, I could tell, but still a bit careful with me, as he had been senior year. He seemed more tense in general.

There was a brief reception in his living room, where perhaps a dozen students who'd shown an interest in writing sat around me in an intimate circle on the floor.

They asked the usual questions, but then one of them said he was writing stories and not showing them to anyone. "Why not work with Cipher?" I said. "He sure taught me a lot."

"With *him?*" Incredulity. It was as if he had not heard my public thanks.

"Yes. Sure." The students raised their eyebrows and exchanged quick glances. They were too polite to go any further. It was the first hint, I suppose, but even after many years my loyalty to the man was too strong for me to press the issue. I let it pass and held my memories.

Years went by. Once or twice, when I'd published a story, I'd send it along to him, but he never responded. Many more years went by, and then my eldest son applied for admission to the college. I have only recently learned that he and his mother (my ex-wife) dropped in on Professor Cipher at his house on campus for a quick visit before my son made his final decision. The interior of the house was apparently a shambles, and Cipher led them through quickly to the back porch. He was polite but "befuddled," as my son put it. "An awkward meeting." Cipher did not, of course, remember my ex-wife, whom he had not seen since she was an undergraduate, and appeared in any case to be under stress, quite possibly already into the whiskey despite the early hour (ten A.M.). On their way out, they met Cipher's daughter—one of a great brood of children, all the rest boys—who apologized for the mess. She had just arrived to clean things up, she said. It was understood she no longer lived there.

Cipher's wife had left him, the children had left him, and I can imagine the depth of his distress. Probably most of the readers of this piece have had their lives fall apart at some time. (My own certainly did, but when it happened I was a good deal younger than Cipher, which made it, presumably, somewhat easier to start over. Perhaps five years for me to reach reasonably stable ground.) In his big, empty house in a corner of the beautiful, sylvan campus—woods, ponds, sweeping lawns—Professor Cipher was in bad trouble. He'd lived there almost his entire adult life, and I have a feeling he didn't know where to turn, except perhaps to the liquor cabinet.

He managed to keep teaching—perhaps he even clung to it—with occasional streaks of brilliance, according to a number of his students, but over the next few years he gradually slid into just going through the motions. Especially in the literature courses.

In 1984, my son's junior year, a group of students published an attack on Professor Cipher in the campus newspaper. His classroom maunderings and unpredictability were objected to in strong terms. The students stopped short of any reference to the rumors that he was an alcoholic, but they were particularly perturbed by his grading, which seemed to them unfair, based on no visible principles, arbitrary and irrational. In the Reagan years, grading was taken very seriously. A number of students had had enough of Professor Cipher, and they wanted him removed.

And so it went for a couple of months. Letters of attack, letters of support (better written and more carefully thought out, by and large), in what might be described as a splendid example of student activism or a tawdry mess, depending on how you looked at it. I was tempted to write a letter, but in the end I thought it might be better if Professor Cipher had the option to believe I was unaware of the whole matter (if indeed, in the midst of the ugliness, he ever thought of me).

I went back to the college for my son's graduation. At the start of the official proceedings, there was a sort of informal procession of the faculty across the lawn toward a small stand of trees near the dining hall. I had been trying to find Professor Cipher for half an hour, moving through family groups, saying hello to a couple of old teachers who remembered me, wandering past platforms and banks of folding chairs, but without success. So I stood under the trees and waited for him.

Young teachers marched in groups of three or four. Old professors, deans and administrators came two abreast. Chatting, laughing, enjoying the perfect spring day. And then there he was, walking alone at a terrific clip, passing people without acknowledging them, as if he were being chased. When he raised his head, I was frightened. Florid from booze, his face was also radiant with anger, exasperation, and somewhere deep in there, behind the fixed lines of almost apoplectic rage, I saw shame. His expression was set—like a mask—and when he looked up and saw me, recognized me, there was the briefest flicker of change, as if he were trying to put on a smile that couldn't make it. Twenty years before, his face had been extraordinarily mobile, wonderfully expressive, with subtle moods and emotions varying from moment to moment, but now it seemed fixed as a gargoyle's.

"Professor Cipher," I said.

"Ah, yes. Conroy. Good to see you. We should sit for a moment."

I knew instantly that my presence made him uncomfortable.

We sat on opposite sides of an outdoor table, Cipher seeming to gather himself to cope with some mild ordeal. Someone put a tray on the end of the table and moved on. A pitcher of punch. Little paper cups. Cipher did not even glance in that direction, but seemed to be studying his clasped hands. We talked about some of the new buildings on campus. Cipher, a practicing Quaker, stated that his long-standing opposition to the compulsory student attendance at Fifth Day Meeting had helped to end that pernicious policy. I started to mention my teaching.

"Still writing?" he interrupted.

"Oh, yes. I had a pretty bad patch there for a while, but writing, oh, yes. Journalism when I had to."

"Nothing wrong with that."

"Things are going much better now."

He nodded. The rest was small talk. He got up and left as soon as he decently could, his face twisting back into the mask the moment he moved away.

Some years later he retired. I wrote him a letter telling him how grateful I was to have been his student, that I never could have written my book *Stop-Time* so young had it not been for my early training with him, and that my teaching was based on his teaching. He never answered, and that did not surprise me.

I began teaching late in life. Forty, broke, unemployed and in debt, I accepted an offer to come to Iowa and the well-known Writers' Workshop more from a sense of desperation than any deep conviction that I'd know what to do when faced with a roomful of young writers. I was, in fact, apprehensive. But the moment I held a student's story in my hand I began to hear the voice of Professor Cipher speaking through my mouth, the ideas, approach and editing techniques of Professor Cipher moving through my mind. The students were in their mid-twenties—far more sophisticated than I had been at eighteen—yet I could tell that no one had line-edited them, no one had talked to them about basic conventions, strategies and the inescapable pressure of the reader's intelligence and imagination. ("Think of the *reader,* sir!") My first workshop was made up of some wonderfully talented people—a great many of whom have since published—and I happily embraced the job. Indeed, I have not stopped teaching since, and I'm convinced one of the reasons I continue to like it so much is that I started so late.

It was good that as an adult I had carefully examined the dynamics of my own youthful projections onto Cipher, because that allowed me to deal better with the phenomenon when, now and then, a student would temporarily project onto me. For some young writers, it is no more than a necessary stage and should be handled with respect, tact, as much measured generosity as can be managed and, of course, common sense. There is no need to back off quite as much as Cipher had backed off from me. (Despite the negative delivery, it was yet another valuable lesson gleaned from the master.) Maybe projection was touchier for Cipher because he had started teaching very early; maybe that was part of it.

My old roommate and I sat in the back of the meetinghouse. This was the place where I had (discreetly) first read Shakespeare's sonnets, the Psalms and other sections of the Bible, as well as Blake's *Songs of Innocence and Experience.* This was the place where I sometimes pondered one of Cipher's offhand remarks about God: "He certainly exists; we know at least that much." I had taken Quakerism more seriously than most of my fellow students.

The room began to fill. Some familiar faces but mostly new ones, since much time had passed and the college itself had doubled in size. Then, from a side door, the family entered. His sons, all of them, looked remarkably like their father. Young men with Swinburne chins, coarse, curly black hair and fleshy lips. I silently hoped that the genes for intelligence had passed through as powerfully as those for appearance. Their mother came in behind them, and they took their places down front.

Quaker meeting, and by extension a Quaker memorial, is free of formal ritual. Everyone comes in, the doors are closed, silence descends, and then anyone who is moved to speak simply stands up and does so. The silence, on this occasion, lasted for some time.

An older dean got up and said that Cipher had been very generous with his ideas about how to improve policy and had often written long letters filled with detail. Someone else said he had been very helpful with the college library. Three or four people told light personal anecdotes, provoking once or twice some gentle, faintly mocking laughter. There was another long silence, and I began to be afraid that no one was going to say anything of substance.

One of the sons stood up and testified that his father had been an impossible man, and intellectually dishonest to boot. "He set up his computer so it could spit out long paragraphs in explanation of his markings"—I immediately thought of awk, cli, unc, and the rest—"and then laughed and said the beauty of it was each student would think he had written it in response to the student's own paper." The young man looked around, arms extended, palms up, as if appealing to the meeting to condemn this outrage. His very confidence put me on alert. In the same way that sometimes, as you go into a house, you can feel that once, in the indeterminate past, something dreadful occurred within its walls, so I suddenly sensed the possibility of animus on a grand scale within this meeting. And there it was. "He was not a modest man," Cipher's sister said forcefully and sat down. One after another, people got up to throw some pebble of complaint, until it seemed a tribal casting-out, a disassociation, a stoning. What kind of monster had he become to elicit this?

When I stood up and repeated, more or less, what I had written to Cipher when he'd retired, when I said a few kind words about him, the whole long line of Cipher heads turned and watched me as if I'd just wandered in from some rest-home field trip. (I was studiously avoided during the brief wine-punch reception after the meeting.)

The last speaker was the college psychiatrist. He said that there was no "healing" in this meeting. It was far too soon. He spoke with the kind of charismatic, fire-and-brimstone certitude I associate with evangelism. "Too many angry words"—he was describing Cipher—"a legacy of words that hurt, that cut, that wound. Too much damage done for any healing here, too much pain." (I paraphrase. What he actually said was probably worse, given my inability at the time to process fully what I was hearing.) As we walked to the parking lot, my old roommate said, "Well, you saved it."

"It didn't feel like it," I said. "It didn't feel like it." In fact, I could hardly think, so deep was my confusion.

Back in Iowa, back to teaching and writing, back to the calm, reassuring routines of domestic life, I was nevertheless haunted for many months by the memorial service. Somewhat obsessively, I kept turning it over and over in my mind, as if through some small, overlooked facet I would be able to make sense of it all, to resolve it. I have not been able to do so. Not even in the writing of this piece, which may well make some readers wonder why I've written it at all.

Perhaps to let Professor Cipher go. I knew him only briefly, a very long time ago, and I must defer to those who knew him all the way through. He became some sort of monster, it seems, and despite his importance to me, my frozen memories do not necessarily redound to him any more than to myself. I sank him in amber, so to speak, and I see now that it was not only from loyalty but from a certain blind vanity as well. So be it. I have let him go.

And so too have I let go my youthful respect for that particular Quaker meetinghouse, and my faith in the purity of the spiritual communion of that particular Society of Friends. He was with them for forty years, and yet not a single voice was raised suggesting more might have been done to help him. No one suggested that any "Friend" in that room shared the remotest iota of responsibility for what had happened to the man. In the face of his death, they were—there is no other word for it—smug.

I am thrown back to Professor Cipher's belief in God. He was young then. I don't know what he believed at the end, nor am I at all sure of what I myself believe. Nevertheless, I wholeheartedly offer these memories and these words as a prayer. A prayer for Professor Cipher. And the sincerity of my prayer should not be questioned because of the sad fact that there is little else I can do. I mean it, friends. Whatever he became, he was once wonderful, and this is my offering to my teacher.

1994

The Writers' Workshop

A
s far as I know, the term "writers' workshop" first came into use some sixty years ago when Iowa University, with the blessing of the Board of Regents, decided to accept "creative" theses in partial fulfillment of the requirements toward earning certain advanced degrees. Quite a radical idea at the time. Write a string quartet toward a Ph.D. in music. Paint paintings for a master's in fine arts. Mount a ballet for dance, or write a play for theater. Despite the initial scandalization of the academy, the idea spread rapidly and is now commonplace. The words "writers' workshop," describing what all those prose writers or poets were doing in all those university classrooms, may have been chosen more for their reassuring overtones of craft guilds, handmade artifacts and so on, than for any descriptive precision.

Writers' workshops around the country reflect wildly different assumptions about what the work should be, what the goals are and how progress might be measured. Some are simply therapy sessions, attempting to create a warm, nurturing environment in which writers are encouraged to express themselves, release their putative creative energies without fear and see what happens. Some have a political agenda—feminist art, black art, social protest art. Some have an aesthetic agenda—minimalism, realism, metafiction. There are writers' workshops specializing in horror fiction, detective fiction, children's fiction and science fiction. There are workshops that have almost nothing to do with writing, where the texts are little more than an excuse for primal-scream catharsis on the one hand, new-age channeling on the other. So it follows that in talking about a writers' workshop, it must be made clear just whose workshop is under discussion. I will attempt to describe my own at the University of Iowa.

Every Tuesday at 4:30 in the afternoon I meet with about a dozen students. We have all picked up copies of the material we're going to talk about—texts written by the two students who are "up" that week—and have read them several times over the weekend, made editorial comments in the margins and written letters to the authors attempting to describe our reactions to the texts. These letters are quite important, first because they are written before any public discussion and hence are not corrupted by what may be said in class, and second because they tend to be more supportive, more personal and sometimes more trenchant than what the writer of the letter might say in class. Thus if a story is torn apart during workshop, the letters, which are read one week later (since I keep them and read them myself during that time), can work to cheer a student up and encourage more work.

We talk for two and a half hours. The author of the text being examined usually remains silent, which some observers find surprising, but which I encourage. If there is a tension between the writer's intentions for the text and what the text, standing alone, appears actually to be doing to the readers, that is a tension the writer should face, and think about. As well, the writer's temptation to defend his or her work can lead to wasted time.

But let me back up now to the first meeting, when we have no texts before us and I try to give a general sense of what I think our work should be. I announce right away that I reserve the right to be wrong, because not to do so would severely restrict my ability to talk at all. Narrative fiction is complex, judgments can be subjective, tastes differ and rules seldom hold.

I further state that the focus of our attention will be the texts, and our goal will be to expand our awareness of how language functions on the page. We will stop with the text, and resist the temptation to go through it and talk about the author. Remarks, thoughts and reactions to a given piece of writing should be addressed to the room as a whole and not to the author, whose presence, for the rest of us, is superfluous. We are studying the text, what the text really is rather than what the author might have wanted it to be or thought that it was.

The people in my workshop are usually in their late twenties, very bright, exceptionally well read by modern standards, ambitious and in thrall to books and literature. As sophisticated as they are about other people's writing, they are often quite naive about their own, half assuming, for instance, that when they write, their souls are on their pages and that an attack on the page is an attack on the soul. I try to make the point that when the soul is truly on the page, the work has risen past the level at which it makes much sense for us to talk about it. Victory has been achieved, and the work passes over to the attention of students of literature, culture and aesthetics. We, on the other hand (and I include myself), have more immediate goals. We're trying to write better prose and to struggle through whatever we have to struggle through in order to do it. In a not entirely ancillary way, we want to get published, as a confirmation of the value of the work and a partial authentication of the worker in the chosen role of writer. These latter passions are tacitly understood as part of the general background of the workshop, but it soon becomes clear that in only the most minimal sense are they a function of the quality of the work. Better to separate, even if somewhat artificially, the text from the author, and keep our attention on the language.

Chalk in hand, I go to the blackboard and suggest that it might be helpful to think about the relationship between the writer and the reader. A common error is to use the following model of a transportation exchange.

Writer ——————→ Text ◄—————— Reader

The writer creates a story and puts it into a code (language) that is the text. The reader decodes the text and receives the story. Simple transportation from the writer/creator to the reader/witness.

But what really goes on is more complicated. The language statement "yellow pencil" can carry no actual color. The reader must add the color with the mind's eye for the full image to emerge. Likewise, the reader's energy is needed to hear tones of voice in dialogue, to infer information that the text only implies, to make full pictures from the text's suggestive sketches of the physical world, to respond to metaphor, and on up to higher and higher levels. The reader is not a passive witness to, for instance, Hemingway's "Hills Like White Elephants." He or she is pouring energy into the text, which, as a result of severe discipline, has been designed to elicit, welcome and *use* that energy. Indeed, without work from the reader the story doesn't make much sense. (What are they going on about? Where is the train taking her, and what is she going to do there?) So the above model is wiped from the board and another put in its place.

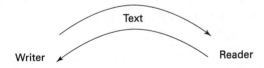

Text

Writer   Reader

This model purports energy from the writer (the act of writing) aimed at the reader, and energy from the reader (the act of reading) aimed at the text. The text is thought of not as a single plane or page in space, but as the zone where the two arcs of energy overlap.

This model suggests that the reader is to some extent the cocreator of the narrative. The author, then, must write in such a way as to allow the reader's energy into the work. If the text is unintelligible, it falls short of the zone and the reader is blocked. If the text is preemptive and bullying, it goes past the zone, smothers the incoming energy, and the reader is blocked. In either case the dance of two minds necessary to bring a living narrative into existence is precluded. Note that no judgment is made about how to handle the reader's energy once it has been allowed in. Great demands can be made of the reader, or lesser ones, depending on what's afoot. The point is, without the active participation of the reader's mind and imagination, nothing will happen. In addition, the model says nothing about the degree or intensity of the energy from the two sides in relation to each other. Obviously it takes *much* more energy (and time) to write good prose than it does to read it.

All right, the students say, assuming we buy the idea of the zone for the moment, what can you tell us about getting into it, or writing toward it? I respond that that is what we will be doing all semester, and that in preparation I will put forward some unproven but possibly useful ideas.

Most writers began writing as an extension of their love of reading. They were excited by books even as children, perceiving a kind of magic going on in narrative which they were eventually drawn to emulate. As they grew older they plunged into literature and became used to reading over their heads. They *eagerly* read over their heads. When, as adults, they try to write, they are often as much preoccupied with magic—effect, simile, metaphors, mood—the fancy stuff—as with meaning. They are intoxicated with the seemingly endless power of language, an intoxication that can be dangerous. For while it is true that reading over one's head is good, writing over one's head is very bad indeed. An almost certain guarantee of failure, in fact.

When we write we are not alone, starting everything from scratch, however much it might feel that way. Literature is a continuum—moving and changing, to be sure—but much has already been done for us. Conventions have been established. When we make paragraphs, use punctuation, follow (flexibly) the rules of grammar and so forth, we are borne by the flow of that continuum. We can employ an omniscient third-person narrator without having to explain who is narrating, because Flaubert and others cleared that particular problem away. A tremendous amount has been done for us. Literature is a river, full of currents and crosscurrents, and when we write, we are in it, like it or not. If we grow too forgetful, we can drown.

At the blackboard again, I draw the following box.

Meaning	Sense	Clarity

This is the first order of business in trying to write toward the zone, the first signal to the reader that his or her energy is welcome, the first announcement of a common ground.

1. Meaning. At the literal level, the writer's words must mean what they say. The author, having chosen them, must stand fully and firmly behind them. *Obese, fat, chubby, heavy* and *stout,* for instance, have different meanings. They are not interchangeable. *He sat down with a sigh* means that the sitting and sighing are happening at the same time, which precludes a construction such as *"I'm too tired to think," he said as he sat down with a sigh.* The reader will undoubtedly get the drift and will separate the sighing from the saying, but the writing is sloppy from the point of view of meaning. It doesn't, at the literal level, mean what it says. Errors of meaning are quite common in lax prose, and there are more ways of making them than I can list here.

2. Sense. The text must make sense, lest the reader be excluded. *The boy ate the watermelon* makes sense. *The watermelon ate the boy* does not, unless the author has created a special world in which it does. Unmotivated behavior in characters doesn't make sense to the reader, who is also confused by randomness, arbitrariness or aimlessness in the text. The writer must recognize the continuous unrelenting pressure from the reader that the text make sense. It can be strange sense, to be sure, but the reader has to be able to understand the text to enter it.

3. Clarity. Strunk and White tell us not to use ten words where five will do. This is because the most compact language statement is almost always clearer than an expansive one. The goal is not brevity for its own sake but *clarity.* The reader expects the writer to have removed all excess language, to have distilled things to their essences, whether the style is simple or complex. If the writer has not done this work, the reader is less enthusiastic about putting energy into the text, less sure about being on common ground. As well, clarity has aesthetic value all by itself. To read Orwell is to get real pleasure from the clarity of the prose, and this is true whether or not one agrees with the politics that are so often embedded in his work.

The struggle to maintain meaning, sense and clarity is the primary activity of any writer. It turns out to be quite hard to do, demanding constant concentration at high levels, constant self-editing and a continuous preconscious awareness of the ghostly presence of a mind on the other side of the zone. Many enthusiastic inexperienced writers (even some experienced ones) would like to skip this struggle, or evade it while maintaining that of course it has some importance but the real action occurs at higher levels, up where the fancy stuff is, the stuff that so moves them as readers. I maintain that any attempt to write from the top down will likely fail. I put forward the idea of a sort of pyramid

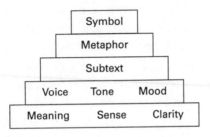

in which the higher levels have a chance to become operative only as the levels below become operative. The most common error ones sees in talented young writers is the attempt to work from the top down rather than the bottom up. A good workshop can save people a tremendous amount of time if it can correct this error. The pyramid is reductive, no more than a thought experiment, really, but it strengthens writers. A great deal of what makes good writing is mysterious and beyond our power to control directly, but we need not be entirely helpless in our attempts to approach the state in which we might possibly increase our chances of doing good writing. You cannot really teach a baseball player how to become a great hitter, says Kurt

Vonnegut, with regard to teaching writing, but you can teach him where to stand in the box, how to shift his weight during the swing, how to follow through and a dozen other things he'll need to know before he can become even a good hitter.

Against this background, then, we begin to look at student texts. Everyone is warned that my remarks are likely to be negative, that experience has shown me that my positive remarks aren't likely to have the same impact, which is too bad, but seems to be the case. I will search out every weakness in the prose that I can, explaining as carefully as I can precisely why I consider each discovered weakness to be an actual weakness, rather than some idiosyncratic response to the text of my own. I will tear the prose apart until I get prose sufficiently strong that it does not tear. This approach creates a good deal of nervousness in the students at first, but as the semester progresses the problem eases. They begin to see the texts are being looked at, not the authors, and that the process is oddly impersonal (especially if it's someone else's work under discussion) and generally rational. We put to the test my assertion that if there is some large, abstract problem with a story, or a series of problems— "It's thin." "It lacks energy." "It lacks narrative drive." "It's frustrating to read." Etc., etc.—the seeds of the problem can *always* be found at the microlevel of language, the words and sentences on the page. That is at least a place for the author to start actual work to strengthen the story rather than simply throwing up one's hands in despair. Another draft, and then again another draft, until one has gone as far as one senses one can reasonably go.

Much of this work has to do with meaning, sense, clarity and working from the bottom up vis-à-vis the pyramid. We spend time and effort trying to find out what's wrong, leaving it to the author to fix it. (Again, some observers find this surprising. My own feeling is that, in prose, any given problem is likely to be susceptible to many different solutions, and that the author's solution is the one that counts. And writing even a simple sentence should be done slowly and carefully within the context of the whole narrative, and never off the top of one's head in a classroom.) I often use the class as a sort of panel to verify the existence of a problem. "How many of you thought they were still in the kitchen, when it turns out they were in the living room?" (We don't vote—it's a question of nodding heads.) If there is a consensus, we go to the language to find out why we thought they were still in the kitchen. If this sounds trivial, we should remember Virginia Woolf's comment after being asked how her three hours of writing had gone one afternoon. (I paraphrase.) "Very well. I got them through the French doors and out onto the patio." She was quite serious.

As we read closely and compare our readings, many kinds of problems can be seen to crop up in the texts. We learn the danger of giving the reader insufficient information—how the reader will simply make something up to fill the vacuum. "You mean they were brothers? I thought they were gay lovers and that's why the macho bartender got on their case." We talk about the Loose Reader, who is able to create the most fantastic cathedrals in the air out of the smallest slips of the author.

We discuss matters of technique and of craft. "This is a first-person story told by Lucy, and since she never went to the trial, how can she know all this stuff about the quality of the light coming through the courtroom window?" We ruminate on the seductiveness of the first person, how it seems easy initially but subsequently becomes very hard. We look at texts in which the author seems trapped in the first person, unable to find a way to look around the narrator, or rise above the narrator. We discuss strategies to avoid such pitfalls.

Inevitably we will come upon a text that is hiding in abject naturalism, where the author creates chronological lists of events rather than selecting some events over others. "I don't know what is important in this story. I don't know what I'm supposed to be paying attention to because everything is treated the same. I mean, all this stuff could happen, but what's the point? What am I supposed to make of it?" The question is rhetorical, of course, because if the text doesn't answer it, it doesn't get answered. The text stands alone, without an explicator, as it does in life.

Because writing is an extension of reading, and because the students have been reading all their lives, it is understandable that the two activities might blur somewhat in their minds. Although it is certainly a good thing that their writing is informed by their reading—indeed, at the most basic level they wouldn't be able to write anything at all if it weren't—it has its dangers. The creation of metaphors and similes, for instance. "The boy hopped up and down," writes a bright student whose intuition, sense of rhythm and experience as a reader tell her a metaphor or simile is needed to complete the sentence, "like beads of water on a hot frying pan." In the rush to meet the demands of intuition and rhythm she has written a weak metaphor. She has forgotten the function of the device, which is to make something crystal clear, to reduce to essence. She has tried to *amplify,* to *add on,* rather than reduce.

Consider John Banville's description of a sound from a very young, practically newborn infant. "In his cot the child made a sound in his sleep like a rusty hinge being opened." He could have stopped with "sleep," but he particularized the sound, reduced it, as it were, by bringing in the rusty hinge (creating a frisson of recognition for anyone who's had a child). John Updike's comparison of the Colosseum to "a ruined wedding cake" is a visual reduction of great power. The point is these experienced writers understand the function of metaphor and simile. The bright student did not. She allowed the reader in her, the mimetic reader, to supersede the writer in her at the moment of composition. Once again, it is up to the student to devise a solution to the hopping-boy sentence. The workshops cannot teach the magic of making thrilling metaphors, but they can at least discuss their function, what it is they're supposed to be doing. Precision.

A problem that sometimes comes up is a narrative that looks like a story—controlled language, dialogue, description, some kind of plot or shape—but is in fact only a mimetic stringing together of various devices that the writer has absorbed as a reader. I do not mean copying, I mean empty writing. Techniques learned while reading narratives that are actually about something are applied in the creation of texts whose raison d'être is nothing more than the re-creation of the techniques for their own sake. Lacking any emotional or intellectual engine, pressure or emerging reason why the reader should continue to read, such texts are stillborn. Happily, this is most often a short phase for young writers, but it can require a good deal of energy to get past it. In truth, writing is a mixture of knowing what you're doing and not knowing what you're doing. John Cheever once told me he never knew how any of his short stories would end, and had to discover the ending and how to get there while in the act of writing each one of them. So even to a master it is not an unknown experience to look down at what you've written, decide it looks like a story and go forward on faith. The author creates the text, and the text whispers to the author, but for this to happen there must be pressure—the text must be in the service of something, even if the author is not yet quite sure what that something is—there must be forward momentum. Mimetic texts are invariably static. Neither do they whisper what they want to become.

The workshop cannot tell or teach a student what his or her text should be in the service of. Such presumption would be outrageous. It wouldn't work in any case. If the text is to have pressure, it must be the author's pressure, which can only come from inside.

Many elements of good narrative fiction cannot be directly learned in a workshop. Narrative drive, metaphor, depth of characterization, wit, dynamics of pitch, humor, narrative authority and a dozen other things are too complex to be broken down intellectually. We should talk about them—talk around them—when they come up in a text, but I suspect that in the end it is the intuitive preconscious forces at work in the writer that matter the most, a certain tense alertness to language being perhaps the most basic. Workshops can help students to dare to trust intuition, or at least lessen their fear of it. Experienced writers know Hemingway was correct when he said the larger part of the iceberg is hidden under the water, and they know that when they are doing their best work, more is going on than they can consciously describe. So be it. The art lifts the artist.

Art cannot be made by committee. Any such use of a workshop will be counterproductive. Thus the student who is "up" should not be looking for solutions from the other students or from the teacher. The student should be looking for problems in the text that he or she had not been aware of. In a good workshop this becomes clear in a matter of hours. (Failure to understand this has led to many a canard from uninformed commentators about what they imagine to be going on at Iowa —the existence of an "Iowa short story," for example, or the assumption that a prevailing aesthetic or style exists that is drummed into the students. Not so. The Iowa Workshop attempts to respond to what each student brings, and each student is unique. The briefest look at the variety in the work of the students—to say nothing of the famous graduates—is the proof.)

Neither can art be made by learning a set of rules and applying them, as is the case, say, with plane geometry. The young writer may well be guided by hints or suggestions that might look like rules, but are in fact only observations not meant to be applied universally. I am reminded of working on a tune with the late jazz musician Paul Desmond—myself on piano and the master on saxophone. At one point, improvising the voicings as I moved from one chord to another, Paul stopped the music, leaned over the keyboard and showed me a better way to do it. "Usually," he said, "but not always, we try to retain all notes common to both chords." Exactly so in a writing workshop. Suggestions are made in that spirit—"usually, but not always."

The workshop concentrates on matters of craft, as it should, but hints, suggestions and thought experiments flow continuously through the semester, offerings whose usefulness is privately determined by each student. Here is a list—notes jotted down by one of my students over a period of three weeks—suggestive of the sorts of things that come up: "Characterization is built not through repetition but through layering . . . The text should imply, so the reader can infer . . . Dramatization is crucial. Too much telling infantilizes the reader . . . The text informs to alert the writer as to its manifest destiny [Cheever!] . . . Written dialogue is very different from spoken, or 'real' dialogue . . . degraded language can degrade a character . . . A text must not have amnesia, each sentence should be linked to all that came before . . . Rhythms should vary," and so forth and so on. These are observations of my own, springing from the discussion of various student texts. Part of the workshop experience is older writers working with younger writers, a sort of atelier where the older writers, who have presumably produced significant work, imply that they have "been there" about some issue, and put forward thoughts for what they are worth. Students seem eager for such information, and I've sometimes wondered if they are not in fact training me to give it, so quickly do they reach for their pens when I get into that mode. I do believe they understand that the value, if any, of such observations lies in their ability to expand the way one thinks about certain problems, rather than their efficacy in immediately solving them.

Many good things happen outside the classroom. At Iowa, the students are in residence for two years in what is for almost all of them a mildly exotic environment: a calm college town in the Midwest where they tend to eat in the same restaurants, go to the same bars, theaters, concerts and grocery stores. They get to know each other very well, and many of them find two or three contemporaries who prove to be particularly sensitive, smart and sympathetic readers. A good deal of discussion about one or another text goes on in coffeehouses, over e-mail or the telephone as a student tries out a couple of paragraphs at one o'clock in the morning. (Allan Gurganus, for instance, found some special readers when he was a student here years ago whom he still consults.) The value of this interplay cannot be overstated, and may well be a critical factor in the integration of whatever may have been learned in class.

At Iowa, young writers get to work with at least four different teachers during the course of their stay. Each teacher has his or her own approach, using methods only indirectly connected to the others', so that the students become aware that the process is more circular than linear. But a common theme is that the students be focused on process rather than project. Students tend to cling to the texts that got them into the workshop in the first place, deeply and understandably worried that the magic might not strike again, that the magic is unpredictable. They mistakenly think that only their strong work is significant and that their weak work is a total waste of time. They fear being exposed as impostors.

The workshop asserts that it is process that counts. All the work is necessary to move ahead, hence it is all valuable. Every writer creates weak, middling and strong work. No one ever knows when lightning will strike, and we are all, much of the time, waiting for it. But we are not passive. We write, we struggle, we take risks. We work to be ready for the lightning when it comes, to be worthy of it, to be able to handle it rather than be destroyed by it. (Success has ruined more writers than failure.) Writing, sayeth the workshop, is a way of life. You either sign on or you don't.

1999

The House of Representatives and Me

GEORGE ORWELL was offended by the imprecise use of language. His sensitivity to the evils of cant, jargon, evasiveness and verbal sloppiness was not limited to the written word. Remember the man in the cafeteria in *Nineteen Eighty-four* talking nonsense? Duckspeak? Quackspeak? Language that sounded as if it meant something but actually didn't? It was great fun to watch Orwell skewer various fatheads, academics, upper-class Brits and blowhards in his wonderful essay "Politics and the English Language." Hoisted on their own petards, they were, and more power to George. He was a hero of mine even before I started to write, and then of course later, when I began wrestling with language in earnest, I cherished him all the more. I still cherish him. About the written word he was entirely correct, but the dynamics of the spoken word may be more complex than he allowed. I began turning the matter over in my mind when, during the Reagan administration, I became a government bureaucrat as director of the literature program at the National Endowment for the Arts in Washington, D.C.

I remember being warned by a wise old gent in Boston who had worked at high levels "inside the beltway" that I wouldn't understand what was going on for at least six months. This turned out to be true. I walked away from many conversations and group meetings at headquarters with a vague sense of unease, feeling I'd missed something, a tacit frame of reference I couldn't quite pick up, like a man who doesn't get a joke. But no one seemed to mind, or, for that matter, notice. I had work to do in any case, getting the taxpayers' money out to what was called "the field" (writers, nonprofit publishers, service organizations and so on) with the help of panels made up of some of the most interesting writers and literary professionals in the country. I always understood what they said, which bolstered my morale.

I was largely at sea during my first visit to the hearings on the NEA before the House Subcommittee on Interior Appropriations—the big, high-ceilinged room jammed with three or four hundred observers. Lobbyists, reporters, arts administrators and the like sat in the back. In front, the Chairman of the Endowment, his satellites, agency staff and a couple of dark suits from the White House, watching to make sure everybody stayed within the President's budget. "No whining! Stay inside the reservation," our Chairman had told us in a staff meeting.

Representative Sidney Yates, a Democrat from Chicago, chairman of the subcommittee and a wise and distinguished old man, had, as it turned out, his own agenda. Since the inception of the Endowment under President Kennedy (signed into law by Lyndon Johnson), Yates had been its most dedicated and powerful protector. He ran the proceedings in a relaxed, genial manner from the raised area at the end of the room. Other members of the subcommittee might come and go, speak briefly into their microphones to put themselves on record or ask a question before disappearing out the side doors, but Yates remained in his leather chair all day, attentive and patient, a model of civility as he questioned one witness after another. I wanted very much not to make a fool of myself. I wanted to please him, if I could only figure out what was going on.

As he interviewed other program directors he seemed to

range all over the place, moving from one area to another without any obvious logical connecting thread. "Well, how are things in the dance program?" he might ask, giving the witness an opportunity to speak about almost anything. Then, abruptly, he might turn to technical matters. "Any progress on the electronic transcription of choreography?" Or he might speak spontaneously about a ballet he'd seen on television and how much he'd enjoyed it.

"Where's he going?" I asked a young lobbyist sitting beside me. "What's he after?"

"Language. He's sort of trolling around for language he can excerpt and use in his report asking the House for more money."

"Oh." I stole a glance at the President's men. One of them appeared to be dozing with lowered head, fingers on brow. The other was covertly reading the *Washington Post.*

"Literature," I remember Sidney Yates saying as I took my place before the microphone. "The foundation of culture. Good afternoon, Mr. Conroy. It's a pleasure to have you with us."

"Good afternoon, sir. A pleasure to be here."

We rambled on about one thing or another in the world of books, various activities in my program, the importance of reading in the lives of children and so forth. It was like a pleasant chat with a favorite uncle, and I grew more and more at ease. Just as my testimony was winding up, after I'd read some statistics into the record, Yates came in very fast, almost interrupting me. "Your program could use some more money, wouldn't you say?"

I stared at him like the proverbial deer caught in the headlights. Yates stroked the side of his head and gave me a sly wink.

"I guess we could always use it, sir," I said. "But I'm not asking for it. I'm not supposed to."

Modest laughter from the audience. A nod from Yates. A thin

smile from my boss, the Chairman. I got up from the witness table. Yates gave me a friendly little wave goodbye. I did not see him again for a year.

The room was the same, the cast was the same. But Yates was more formal in his tone, more focused. The following dialogue is from the *Congressional Record*. It does not make for fascinating reading, but it was not supposed to. Nobody (but me) was supposed to pay much attention.

Mr. Yates: Mr. Conroy, you had 1,870 applications in 1981; 441 grants. You went way up in 1982 to 2,632 applications and a few more grants, 456. You are being cut back in 1983 and the number of grants is 326.

Mr. Conroy: Those figures represent poetry and prose. We always get more applications—

Mr. Yates: What else is there in literature?

Mr. Conroy: What I mean to suggest is that they all terminate. The first figure in front of you was prose for 1981. The next figure is poetry. That is always a large figure. We got more poets asking for grants. The third figure is back to prose again because it alternates.

Mr. Yates: I see. What effect will the reduction in the budget have upon you?

Mr. Conroy: Well, we are not getting as severe a reduction as some of the other programs. There will be less activity on fewer grants.

Mr. Yates: You are being cut by 16 percent.

Mr. Conroy: Yes.

Mr. Yates: Is 1983 your year for prose or poetry?

Mr. Conroy: Prose.

Mr. Yates: So the poets will have to wait for 1984.

Mr. Conroy: Yes, indeed.

Mr. Yates: What are they going to do?

Mr. Conroy: Spread out the money that they got. Essentially, they are two-year grants.

Mr. Yates: Oh, they are?

Mr. Conroy: Well, that is the way it works out because you apply on alternate years.

Mr. Yates: How much of a grant do you make? Do you make a grant sufficiently large to cover two years?

Mr. Conroy: No. The grant is $12,500.

Mr. Yates: They are going to have to husband their resources.

Mr. Conroy: Yes, indeed.

So, there it is. Innocuous on the surface, but containing at least the faint suggestion of a strategy to sneak off the reservation so quietly that no one would notice until it was too late. Yates provided the seed, and although I do not claim to have grasped the whole beautiful scheme in a moment, I saw enough to move forward at each stage. Yates and I put it together right in front of everybody—the Chairman, various White House watchdogs, the press and even the other subcommittee members. It was my most powerful lesson in government. Talk at a remove or two. Think subtext. Victory comes through stealth and tenacity.

I asked that the grants be raised to $20,000, while we would award fewer of them so that the action would be budget neutral. (The magic words! Guaranteed to put certain subjects into a trance.) A year later, when everyone had forgotten what we'd done, Yates and I got into a long, soporific analysis of various statistics, and he was shocked—shocked!—to discover how the ratio between the number of applicants and the number of grants awarded had eroded so drastically over the years. I agreed it was a sad fact and ended my testimony, keeping a straight face.

Now the usual procedure for funding an agency like the National Endowment for the Arts was for the money to be sent to the Chairman, who would then distribute it as he saw fit to the various programs and administrative units. But Yates, a true believer in the arts, did not completely trust the Chairman, who was a lawyer and a bit of a dilettante when it came to artistic matters. And Yates was a powerful man—the Dean of the House, many called him—with special privileges few people knew about. After the traditional funding had taken place, Yates sent the Chairman an additional million dollars with specific instructions that it be given to the literature program to allow for an increase in fellowships.

Line item! Line item! I thought the Chairman was going to have a stroke at this outrageous power grab. It was *his* power, after all, which he, like everyone else in Washington, protected with a tenderness usually reserved for the most vulnerable parts of one's body. "It is against the law, Conroy," he said. "You are not allowed to lobby Congress. You can't go and make a deal with Yates behind my back! You shouldn't even be talking to him!"

I told the Chairman that I had never exchanged a word with Yates except at the hearings. I had never spoken to him on the telephone or corresponded with him in any way. I protested my innocence. "I never spoke to the man outside your presence." It was the truth, although I could see how it might be uncomfortable for the Chairman to believe it. In any case, for this and other reasons, he fired me six months later. "Time for a change," he said.

Yates and I were talking a kind of Duckspeak, but there was something hidden underneath. To recapitulate: In the testimony, Yates introduces ratios of grants to applications as something he might play with in his search for language to present to the House. (He is free to leave out, if he chooses to do so, the fact that the genres alternate year by year.) I speak of the grants as two-year grants, giving him something to play with. (Specious logic, since the grants go to different people each cycle. It's money—time has nothing to do with it.) Yates suggests that the grants are too small, thereby suggesting that I use the old chestnut and suggest that they haven't been corrected for inflation in a long time. (Which is what I did.)

It was weirdly exhilarating for me to use language this way, after a lifetime of doing my best to use it straight. It seemed exotic, like some kind of Oriental mind game. It was, of course, only business as usual. Almost everything spoken in the House and the Senate is done in this fashion, in language that both conceals and reveals simultaneously. As I sat behind my friend Senator Paul Tsongas during the Foreign Relations Committee's session with George Shultz, President Reagan's candidate for secretary of state, I heard it again in the questions and responses. It occurred to me that as a practical matter democracy couldn't function using Orwell's kind of language. It just wouldn't work.

Concealment, if not outright deception, is a necessary part of discourse in all parts of our government except the Supreme Court. When President Clinton split linguistic hairs, applied tortured logic, wiggled and danced in the Monica Lewinsky scandal, many Americans were horrified at his evasiveness, and, as it turned out, his lies. On the other hand, what angered members of the House and Senate was not the way the President was using language—using it the way all politicians must use it— but what he was using it for. Clinton broke the tacit rules—you may conceal to make law or make policy but not to cover a personal peccadillo. After so many years in government, however, it may not be possible for the President to talk straight even if he wanted to. It's a different way of thinking, after all.

2000

Me and Conroy

H E NEEDS ME more than I need him, but you'd never know it from the way he treats me. Contempt is perhaps too strong a word. It's something icier, more distant, more perfectly disinterested. He uses me as if I could easily be replaced, which is certainly not true. Not easily, anyway. Who else would put up with him the way I have? (For instance, this is the fourth version of this manuscript, and it's only a tiny bit better than the first. A lot of time for a very small gain, in other words, and no complaints will be heard.) Who else would ask nothing of him—and I mean nothing, not once, ever—simply for the experience of his company? What makes it worse is I think he knows all this and finds it banal. Yes! He does! I felt it just now as my hand wrote the word.

Should I mention the matter of the cigarettes? I think I should. After smoking a pack a day for forty years, I stopped five months ago. Quitting was difficult, to say the least, but the support of my family and friends helped. I'm on the verge of a big change here, which is to say seeing myself as a nonsmoker, accepting myself as a nonsmoker. Everybody respects this except him. My abstinence irritates him for some reason, and when I try to write he tempts me with images of the red and gold Dunhill package, which he knows I used to smoke on special occasions. "Is this not a special occasion?" he seems to be saying, "with the clipboard across your knees and your pen in your hand? Is this not as special as it's ever going to get?" Arrogant bastard.

You see, there's nothing fancy about it. The situation resembles the story line of a thousand execrable country-western songs more than it does any delicate Borgesian aperçu. I've laid my life on the line, and if that isn't love I don't know what love is. For my entire adult life he has simply popped up whenever it pleased him, used me, put me through a million changes and split without warning, leaving me exhausted and enervated. He takes me, and my love, totally for granted, and if I had any brains I'd tell him to fuck off. But of course it's far too late for that. He is my fate, for better or worse.

I just wish he'd talk to me directly sometimes. You know, stop whatever he's doing and look me in the eye and tell me something that would help me get rid of this idea of myself as some feckless brokenhearted jukebox cowboy crying in my beer. I mean, would the sky fall? Would the stars freeze in their courses? God damn it, he owes me. Don't you think?

1995

More Observations Now

I WAS DRAWN to the piano as a child. At nine or ten years old, alone a great deal, I became engrossed in the sounds coming into the air—as if freed—when I pressed the keys. First the sounds themselves, then the relationships between the notes. The orderliness of the octave system (the basic layout of the keyboard) suggested rationality. My ear alone told me that the fifth note of any scale was the most important, the most fitting, the most blendable, the most natural note when played with the root. After the fifth, the fourth also sounded very good. As if in the grip of some powerful repetition compulsion (and maybe I was), I would play these simple elements hour after hour, listening as intently as a Tibetan monk to the holy sounds of the gongs. After laboriously picking out some left-hand boogie-woogie figures from late-night uptown radio jazz programs, I put it all together and found the simple twelve-bar blues.

I played the blues, moving slowly into easy variations and complications, for years. The blues and nothing else. (It was a good thing I was alone in the house. Anyone listening would surely have been driven mad.) When I found something new— usually in a flurry trying to fit in, or correct for, a mistake—I would work on it for weeks, repeating and repeating. Of course this meant very slow development, and also unbalanced development, in which the physical fascination with sound held me back from exploring notation, scales, harmony (that rationality that the layout of the keyboard not only suggested but contained) and the intellectual satisfactions of really knowing what I was doing.

It seems clear now that if I'd had even a reasonably competent teacher, I would have been pushed to move faster, to let go and move on, to learn to sight-read, but I got instead an angry, sadistic, repressed homosexual who loved to squeeze my skinny neck with his exceptionally strong hands whenever I tried his patience. I went back to playing on my own.

Eventually I got some sheet music and learned my first thirty-two-bar tune. "Tenderly," it was called (unconscious irony in my selection?). Using the "Every Good Boy Does Fine, General Electric Company of America" system, in conjunction with my ear (to resolve questions of meter), I learned the tune and played it several thousand times over the next couple of months.

Therein lay my error. I could not just learn a tune, however slowly, and go on to another one. I had to play it over and over, so many times that it became engraved in the neurons of my brain, the muscles of my arms and hands, the nerves of my fingers. I was walking backwards into the future, as they say.

In a *New Yorker* obituary for Bill Evans, the great jazz pianist, I described how Evans had taken traditional training as a child in Jacksonville, Florida, and subsequently developed what was to become the most influential jazz piano style of his generation by sitting at the piano all day with a stack of music at one end— Chopin, Debussy, Ellington, Liszt, Schubert, in no particular order—and sight-reading his way through until the stack was at the other end. A good way to learn piano, and a good way to learn music. It's what I should have done.

"Well, do it now," suggested a friend, who played Bach on his beautiful recorder and wanted to do duets. "It's a snap. You can learn in a matter of months." He knew I could read two novels a day, and thought I could simply switch over. But as I mention elsewhere in this book, I had gone too far into a physical relationship with the piano by then (this was in the 1960s), so that giving my eyes supremacy over my hands was impossible. In any case, it would not have been a snap; it would have been a good deal of work.

So I played for fun, inching along like a typical autodidact, leaving great gaping holes in my training, and never took any of it very seriously. I played jazz in the house by myself and did not anticipate going any further. But then I met Casey, an Asian tungsten millionaire who owned a restaurant in the Village. There was a Steinway grand up against the brick wall.

"Why don't you play here a couple of nights a week? Say Monday and Tuesday?"

I was more than surprised. I was almost shocked. "I'm not good enough. Not nearly."

"You're okay," Casey said. "I've heard you."

In those days I ran with a pretty glamorous crowd uptown, and he'd heard me fooling around at one club or another, usually on some broken-down spinet. (In retrospect, I realize that Casey, and later Bradley Cunningham, at Bradley's, hired me thinking I might draw people from uptown down to the Village on the traditionally slow nights of Monday and Tuesday. To some extent they were right.)

"But I make mistakes."

"So what?" We were drinking beer at the end of the bar, looking out over the long, deep room. Tablecloths, candles, place settings, sparkling glasses—everything perfect. There was no one there but the waiters. In two hours a hundred people would be eating dinner. He waved to indicate the space. "So you play the wrong note. Who's going to hear it? Who's going to care?" He put his hand on my arm. "Listen. Get yourself a bass player. It'll be good money."

I was scared, but I did it. Two sessions at home with a fine bassist I'd met in Harlem, and we began a gig that was to last a year. For the first month or so I played in a state of mild terror, but Casey had been right—apparently no one heard the mistakes. Nevertheless, I would listen so hard to the bass-piano mix the audience seemed far away, noise in the background, oddly soothing. Eventually I started having some serious fun. It was a completely different story playing with another person, another imagination. It was terrific, and I began to learn at a faster rate than ever before.

Two nights stand out in memory. The first was a fairly crowded Tuesday, as I sat at the piano between tunes. I watched an attractive couple who had just come in, moving through the hubbub to their table. As they took their seats, one of those strange crowd moments occurred. For no reason at all there was an instant of something like silence, an abrupt fall-off which allowed me to hear the man, speaking quietly, say to the woman, "Watch his face." Then the ambient buzz of the crowd returned.

Many players have idiosyncrasies. Erroll Garner, the self-taught jazz pianist, was once asked why he grunted, hummed and growled when he played. "Because I can't play good enough." He couldn't get where he wanted to be with his hands alone. Bill Evans would sometimes play an entire tune so bent over that his head almost touched the keyboard. Glenn Gould drove his engineers to distraction with his muffled singing. Keith Jarrett shouts, laughs and whoops in concert, and he can't stop himself. Jimmy Garrison, the superb bassist, would screw up his face and grimace as if in pain as he played his solos. I knew, sort of, that my face went through all kinds of changes when I was playing, different things happening as a reflexive echo of the music. A good friend of mine once joked that I looked as if I suffered from some exotic nervous disorder. I never cared one way or the other because I was so caught up in the urgency of getting through the tunes. "Watch his face," the guy had said, and I immediately became self-conscious. During the next set I tried to maintain an expressionless mask.

"Hey," the bass player whispered after the second tune, "what the fuck is wrong with you? You sound like a little old lady."

The hell with it, I thought. It doesn't matter if I look like a freak—what matters is the music. I jumped into "Honeysuckle Rose," and took a long bebop solo, faces and all.

"Right on," he shouted from behind my left shoulder. "Now you talking!" So that was that.

Some months later I was at the bar, on my break, waiting for the bass player to return from an errand. We followed the New York schedule pretty closely—forty on and twenty off—but more than half an hour had gone by without music and I was getting nervous. I should point out that playing solo jazz piano is particularly difficult. Without a bass player to free up the pianist's left hand, technical challenges mount up rapidly, and my technical skills were minimal. But after forty minutes I had to do something, so I sat down and began to play midrange chords with my left hand and an improvised line with my right. The tune was "Autumn Leaves."

Sometime in the third chorus a large black man got up from his dinner and moved forward, weaving past the other tables, coming toward me with what seemed to be a sense of purpose. As he approached, I recognized Charles Mingus—the foremost jazz bassist in the world—and I was afraid. Mingus, a manic depressive, was famous for sudden onsets of rage. I had been in the audience at the Five Spot, in fact, on the night he threw his valuable German contrabass through the air and into the brick wall, smashing it to pieces. He was very strong, and now he was upon me.

My friend and colleague's bass was leaning against the piano. Mingus gave me a short nod, picked up the instrument carefully, waited for the top of the tune and began to play with me. I could hardly believe what was happening. (A cliché, yes, but that's what it felt like.) When my regular bass player came back and stood watching us from the bar, he was also slightly stunned. (Suffice it to say he was never late again.) Mingus seemed to be enjoying himself and we played an entire set.

The most important night of my musical life, because I no longer had to think of myself as an impostor. If Charles Mingus got up to play with me, I must have been doing something right. I was no genius, but I was a musician. He had freed me, in a way. And there was a lesson in it, too. You don't have to be great to play jazz. It's okay if you're not great—good, strong, interesting music can be created by even a mediocre instrumentalist.

A year or so later, in another club, Mingus and I split a bottle of his favorite Pouilly Fuissé after he had, once again, sat in with me.

"What's going on, Charlie? You're the best bassist in the world and I'm a putzer."

"You are," he said expansively, "an authentic primitive. That is true." He leaned forward and lowered his voice. "But you swing."

2001

My Harlem

THE SEED was planted early. I can't have been more than six or seven years old when I saw *Dumbo* at the local movie palace on Eighty-sixth Street in New York. Of course movies were very important in the days before television, not only because of the big images on the screen, but because this was also before hi-fi, and hence the sound—especially the music—pouring with such power and clarity from the enormous hidden horns and speakers was an experience unique to that medium. The music seemed to go right to the marrow of one's bones.

Dumbo was fine, Dumbo was all right, but it was the three black crows that did it to me, that got me jumping up and down on my seat in a veritable frenzy of excitement and delight. The sass, the jive, the exquisite mockery, and above all the jazzy music, a wonderful, hot, energetic, celebratory and completely satisfying kind of music which I understood instantly, as if I had known it in a previous life, all of it blended together to unlock previously dormant pleasure centers in my brain and sweep me away in childish ecstasy. Black crows on the screen, but young as I was, I knew what truly animated them: Negro voices and Negro music. The seed was planted.

I got my first radio when I was ten or eleven, a small, cheap affair enclosed in a cardboard case sprayed with some kind of green fuzz. Late at night I would set it up beside my pillow and tune in the uptown stations at the top of the dial, where the voices were black and the music was jazz. Over hundreds of hours, before I knew anything of notation, I absorbed the twelve-bar blues as a musical form—it became (and remains) as natural and inevitable to me as breathing—and began to pick up on the astonishingly wide variety of styles, moods, colors, emotions and energies contained in the music. Since there was a piano in the living room I was already beginning to fool around with, I took special interest in the boogie-woogie of people like Cow Cow Davenport and Meade Lux Lewis, the energetic stride styles of Fats Waller and Earl "Fatha" Hines, and the all-out blaze of eclectic virtuosity of Art Tatum. I heard Basie, Ellington, Cab Calloway, Claude Hopkins, Benny Goodman, Lionel Hampton and dozens of other bands and instrumentalists. My passion was intense and private, since I did not know a soul who listened to the music or was even aware of it. In my childish animism, I believed that some of my love was going back into the radio, back through the aether to the players uptown who had given me so much, back, indeed, to the whole warm, ebullient Negro world which I had constructed in my head, and to which I imagined myself connected. I was lovesick, and the word "Harlem" was emblematic of my condition. Harlem, a land of spiritual milk and honey. When I finally got up there, I found out things were a little more complicated. It was a real place, after all, and not a dream.

I was sixteen, going to summer school to make up for all the high school courses I'd failed, and I met a kid named Earl. Although his main interest was the guitar, he messed around on the piano, and we would cut class and sneak into the music room upstairs and try to play four-hand blues. He invited me up to the projects on Lexington Avenue where he lived with his parents and older sister. It was a close-knit family (in retrospect,

I realize they would have to have been, considering the size of their apartment, all of them fairly fat, jammed in together), but they were generous in their welcome. Earl and I spent most of the time downstairs, hanging out on the street or the pocket playground.

There was curiosity at what a white kid was doing spending the hot summer nights in a completely black neighborhood—sometimes, although rarely, even a hint of hostility in the incredibly fast, dense, elliptical, rhyme- and metaphor-laden language swirling continuously in the air. (Earl sometimes had to translate, although he would also explain, later, that some of the kids laid it on a bit thick because I was white, in a sort of linguistic dramatization of the complexity of their turf.) But I was struck with how Earl's premature description of me as a piano player always worked. Skinny and quiet as I was, it was nevertheless a sufficient entrée. Music was respected by everyone.

I remember a pervasive sense of excitement uptown, although in truth nothing much ever happened except talk. Now and then an impromptu jam might develop, near the benches in the pocket playground—a guitar, pots to play bongo-style, a harmonica, somebody singing scat—but always in an offhand, self-deprecatory manner, as if what was happening was only a reference, an homage, to music. And, too, nobody wanted to play full out, since nobody was very good, and the public announcement of one's limitations would work against the maintenance of one's cool. Talk was the game, and talk had its own music, its own virtuosos, its own cutting sessions. (The now legendary instrumental cutting sessions of bebop players in Minton's and other clubs seem to me logical extensions, divine distillations, of the continuous language games on the street—the jive talk, the dozens, etc.) Nothing much was happening where we were, but the allusive, self-mythologizing, convoluted, cryptically inside flavor of discourse among us kept us all convinced that great and dramatic things were indeed happening, even as we sipped our Cokes, albeit slightly outside the periphery of our direct experience. The very air of Harlem, that vast humming black capital of America, was an intoxicant. When the summer ended I said goodbye to Earl, his family and the rest of the guys and went to Europe.

It was many years before I returned. In Europe I listened to a number of black expatriate musicians—Bud Powell was the most famous, but there were unknown players also—and hanging out with them always caused a rush of homesickness. They showed me, with the generosity so often evident in jazz players, good stuff about the blues. It was in Copenhagen, of all places, that I was taught Charlie Parker's twelve-bar changes, by a black trumpet player from Kansas City. I was gently encouraged to learn how to read music, although no one seemed to hold it against me that I couldn't.

I should have done so in college, a small liberal arts institution outside Philadelphia, where I spent most of my time chasing girls, but it was perhaps in a sense too late even then, since I had developed a direct physical relationship to the piano that I was loath to give up. I could not bring myself to make my hands the slaves of my eyes. I was having too much fun with the blues, which seemed never to run out. I also developed a certain crude adeptness at faking. I played dances and mixers at Bryn Mawr and Swarthmore with a quartet and somehow blundered through the requisite ballads and show tunes by ear. Young, ignorant and defensive, I clung to a stupid pride at playing without knowing what I was doing, as if it made me purer as a jazzman. (Of course it did not; it only slowed what little progress I was able to make and exacerbated a kind of musical tunnel vision.) What saved me, to the extent that I was saved at all, since, as it turned out, I never rose above what Charlie Min-

gus eventually said about me once after we'd played a set together—"an authentic primitive" was the euphemism—what
saved me was the fact that I could swing.

New York City, when I came back in my twenties, was a hot
town. There was jazz all over, great musicians playing, and it
was cheap. All you needed was a car to get around and a few
bucks for beers and sandwiches, and I had both. There were
clubs downtown, and there were clubs uptown.

One night, after the show at the Apollo (now I could actually
go to all the places I'd learned about from Earl and the kids), a
bit revved from the music, I crossed 125th Street and strolled
south on the avenue, enjoying the hustle around me, the feeling
of action, the sense of things in the offing which Harlem still
engendered. As I approached Sugar Ray's, a bar owned by the
original Sugar Ray Robinson, I heard the sound of a sax as
someone came out the door, and on an impulse I went in. A
long, deep room—bar to the left, small round tables against the
wall on the right, some banquettes to the rear, and there, all the
way at the back, a small bandstand. A bald man was playing
tenor with a young-looking kid on drums—funky blues with a
backbeat. The place was crowded, noisy and smoky. There were
no other white people. I moved down to the end of the bar and
found an empty stool. I ordered a beer and swiveled to watch
the musicians. They were playing hard, both faces gleaming
with sweat under the small spotlight. A big Hammond organ
took up one side of the bandstand. I wondered why no one was
playing it.

I had some knowledge of the protocols and procedures of
sitting in. These were delicate matters, and understandably so.
One bad musician on the stand could make everyone sound
bad and look bad. The ideal way to go about it was to spend
some time with the musicians, gossip a bit about the jazz scene,

the big clubs and who was playing where, etc., to establish one's general credentials, while at the same time staying alert for the opportunity to establish one's specific credentials. As in: "You guys play that in G? I should try that, I always play it in F." You had to know what you were talking about, because most players heard a great deal of bullshit in their working lives and were quick to sense it in the air. The two guys on the stand were good —the tenor man particularly—and I planned to approach them on their break. But they ducked through a rear door and disappeared.

I had a couple of beers and bided my time, sitting and listening to the fast talk, laughter and hip patter going on around me. People were having fun, and the place had a terrific feel. I knew perfectly well that Harlem was a slum, filled with poverty and despair, and I had no illusions about the iniquitous economic forces working on these people—many young white men knew that—but I also knew there was a lot of life uptown, a kind of vividness and heat which I relished. No doubt there was some connection between the misery in the side streets and the gaiety on the avenue, but the truth was I didn't think about it. I needed to feel the heady mixture of spiritedness and soulfulness I found in clubs like Sugar Ray's, and had found in the blues for half my life as well. The idea of putting the two together, of actually playing the blues uptown, was irresistible. So when the musicians reappeared, I went to the edge of the stand. The bald sax man gave me a brief, slightly startled glance and then stared off toward the front, jerking his head back in an infinitesimal gesture. I began to frame some question about the Hammond when I heard a soft voice beside me.

"Can I help you?"

He was tall. He was very tall, and slender, dressed in a well-cut dark suit and tie. The bouncer, I thought, but he seemed too thin. Then I noticed how extraordinarily high above his shoulders his head was, and how the steeply rising lines from the points of his shoulders to the base of his neck indicated the presence of a great mass of muscle where most people had only a few strings. He was very dark, not quite aubergine, and about thirty years old. There was a stillness in the way he held himself, a kind of bodily authority.

"I was going to ask to sit in," I said, addressing both the bouncer and the sax player. "I mean if no one's coming. Keep a bass line going."

The bald man ducked his head, scratched his nose, looked at me and then looked at the bouncer. I sensed it was up to the bouncer.

"Man want to play," he said, "let him play." He turned and moved back toward the front.

I waited for a nod from the sax player and then climbed up on the stand and slid onto the bench.

"You use your feet?" he asked, referring to the two octaves of bass pedals below the console.

"No."

He switched on the electricity, flipped a few stop levers and reached across me to depress two black keys in the extreme bass. There was no sound and the keys stayed down. "That doubles the bass," he said. "What you want to play?"

"The blues."

"C jam," he said, and counted off the beat.

And just like that we were in it. I was in it. I found the appropriate volume by depressing the broad pedal under my right foot, and the bass line from my left hand poured through the speakers into the heavy air like hot honey. A powerful sound— not loud, but deep. I was nervous, so I concentrated, listening hard to the crisp, white shattering sounds of the ride cymbal and the high hats, and the smoky, fluid lines of the tenor. After a while I began to pop in a few simple Basie-like chords with my right hand, getting my fingers off fast, as if the keyboard were the surface of a hot stove. We had a groove, and when I looked up to the bald man he gave me a wink over his mouthpiece, turned, bent forward slightly and began to dig into his solo. We had a groove.

To say it felt good is an understatement. The pure glee of the kid jumping up and down on the theater seat was perhaps still the core, an almost painful pleasure made denser because now it was pushing against something—the music itself, the act of playing—but with the added sweetness of knowing it would go on and on. What a moment when he bent forward, and I knew he was going to take off, play dozens of choruses and take me with him! It felt inexpressibly wonderful to be there, to be playing, to be alive. It was heaven.

After half an hour most of the people in the bar were up dancing, bopping or clapping time in the crowded space between the bar and the small tables, a whole column of people from the edge of the stand all the way to the front door in constant motion, some of them shouting up at us. "Yeah! Do it do it do it! Aww-right!" Heads back, white teeth flashing. We played and played, sailing through time, until we could play no more.

Drenched, glowing and utterly spent, utterly cleansed, I made my way to the bar. The bouncer (whose name, as it turned out, was Sonny) stood by the service area. He nodded his head once, just once.

"I had a feeling," he said. "Don't ask me why." Then he turned to the bartender. "Red, give this man whatever he wants. On the house."

Sugar Ray's became my uptown pied-à-terre, a place to play and a place to hang out, in a relationship that was to last many years (into the late sixties, in fact). Sonny, ex-boxer and jazz lover, became a friend, and we'd go up to Small's Paradise and the other clubs on his nights off to hear music and eat good southern food. He knew a lot of people, both on the street and in the clubs, and he introduced me around. Occasionally, if it was after three A.M. and we still felt like drinking, we'd go to an illegal after-hours joint in the basement of a brownstone on 121st off St. Nicholas. I'd thought he was joking when he said people had to check their guns, but I did not laugh when I saw the assortment of hardware on a shelf beside the hat-check girl, each evil-looking revolver or pistol neatly tagged. The place was run by a stunning middle-aged café-au-lait Jamaican named Shirley, who used to tease me incessantly. "Come on now, Frankie," she'd say with a nudge of her elbow, "you know you want it. I've got just the right girl for a shy boy like you. Why don't you speak up, now?" I would decline, politely, and she would laugh, jive me a little more, then let up. (No one called me Frankie, or had ever called me Frankie, except the people I knew uptown.)

I jammed at Sugar Ray's every couple of weeks. I was not paid, but neither could I pay. My glass was never empty. If I dropped in in the afternoon after a ball game at the Stadium, Red would push my money back and start talking about the Yankee pitching staff, the glory days of DiMaggio, boxing, politics or his experiences in the army. Those were pleasant afternoons, the sun streaming through the front windows to reveal the essential seediness of the place, the talk rambling and unhurried, people drifting in, saying hello, drifting out.

I realize now that I was a privileged young man. In those easier times my modest skills as a player had been enough to open an entire world, where I was treated with respect and even affection. How many dozens of times had I walked alone along the dark side streets, three-quarters drunk, dressed up (I always dressed well to go uptown), to get to the all-night stand on Seventh Avenue for a chili hot dog? Not once was I accosted or hassled in any way. Never.

Jarrett

THE PLACE IS a large city in Europe, Japan or the United States. The scene is a concert hall. Thousands of people pour into the building and take their seats. The house lights go down. Onstage, a Steinway grand piano, with its bench. A young man, rather short, with a compact, powerful body, emerges from the wings. His face is sharp and intelligent. Applause rises, then cuts off abruptly as he sits down at the piano.

Thus far, a familiar scene. A piano recital, beginning as piano recitals have always begun. But there is a difference, a fundamental difference of great significance. The young man does not know what he is going to play. He knows what he is *not* going to play—not Chopin, not Bach, not Mozart or Bartók, not any of the others he might very well play in another sort of concert, not the music of Ellington, Strayhorn, Monk or the jazz writers he particularly likes, not even any of his own written music. As he raises his hands to the keyboard, his mind, musically speaking, is a blank. He has been concentrating for the last half-hour on keeping it blank—free of any little scraps of melody, empty of any associations, void of any premature structural or thematic ideas. He goes so far as to attempt to wipe out any intellectual memory of ever having played the piano before, for he is determined, once he starts, to avoid repeating anything he might have played in the past in similar cir-

cumstances. Indeed, his preparation is the exact opposite of
that of all the other young men elsewhere in the world who
might, at that same moment, be sitting down in other concert
halls to play for other audiences. He wants to be empty. What
does he play, then? The only relevant answer is that he plays
music. Totally improvised music.

His hands come down, his fingers strike the keys, and there is
a sound. The sound seems to have a direction and he follows
that direction. He listens. The sound becomes more complex
and his hands begin to roam, opening more music from the
strings of the piano. He is improvising, but not, as we are most
familiar with that art, on a given theme. He simultaneously improvises theme, variation, development and structure. It is all
improvised, made on the spot, from instant to instant. There
would appear to be no other player in the world, from any musical background, who does what he does on the concert stage.
His name is Keith Jarrett.

Jarrett began life in modest circumstances. A large family in Allentown, Pennsylvania. His father worked in real estate, and
money was scarce, but Keith and his four brothers had enough
fun growing up so as not to notice. Keith began playing piano in
1948 at the age of three. His mother encouraged him, and somehow teachers were found. There were no other musicians in the
family as far back as anyone could remember, but the boy unquestionably was a prodigy. By his early teens, he was playing
the classical literature in concerts and recitals.

The psychological pressure of early exposure to large audiences has warped many a promising artist, but Jarrett was quite
strong, even as a child, and through those years one imagines
him growing more and more confident as a performer. (He
would occasionally include his own music in the program—
sketches or small pieces.) At home there was the hard work of

practice, but also the pleasure of going deeper and deeper into music itself. Jarrett has loved music—and loved playing—from the start. The worst threat his mother could make, if she saw him let up at practice, was to sell the piano. He would sight-read omnivorously, playing every composer he came across; by the age of ten or eleven, his technique had developed to the point where he began to feel a certain freedom at the keyboard. In order to improvise as successfully as he later would, he first had to be able to play in all keys easily, modulate effortlessly and not have to worry overmuch about his hands, fingering, runs and so on. He achieved these not inconsiderable feats at a very young age, in part by refusing to narrow his approach to the piano (becoming a Chopin specialist, or the like) and by moving ahead broadly, playing every sort of music.

"I think of my musical evolution from the very beginning as being completely straightforward," Jarrett said recently. "I have moved into various categories when each of those categories seemed to be the closest thing to the music within me." At fifteen, he began to play jazz; its creative possibilities intrigued him. One could improvise in jazz, and Jarrett was drawn to it, even though, at first, it was improvisation over a given structure. He had composed music in one form or another all his life, but the spontaneous, instantaneous nature of modern jazz seemed to represent a special kind of challenge and excitement. He went to the Berklee College of Music in Boston because of its emphasis on jazz, and supported himself playing commercial cocktail music in local bars and hotels. He met jazz musicians, and played with them, and began to build a local reputation as a good player. After a year at Berklee, however, he did not reregister. He felt the school could not teach what he wanted to learn—to improvise creatively. "It's not a particularly creative place," he says now. "It's a trade school, really."

At critical points in his life, Jarrett seems to have made decisions by looking into himself, almost as if he were improvising his life as well as his music. At seventeen, an important honor came his way—the chance to study privately in Paris with Nadia Boulanger, all expenses paid; yet he turned it down. Boulanger was one of the most famous and most admired teachers of composition in the world, and to have been her student would have opened all sorts of musical, professional and academic doors. However, Jarrett was not swayed by the practical considerations—he had already chosen another path. He explains, "I always had a feeling of something special ahead of myself." If he didn't know precisely where his growth would lead him, he sensed the direction at least, and made his choices accordingly.

Given his particular interests, he could hardly have picked a better time to get into jazz. For years most jazz music had been a direct extension of bebop. If a quartet of young players got together in the early sixties to play, chances are something like the following would happen: First they would choose a tune to which everyone knew the chord changes. Those harmonies would be pretty much set, and would indicate the outlines of the figured bass line, the chords for the piano and the scales for improvisation. The drummer would play time—that is to say, the basic meter would remain the same—and improvised melodic lines would overlay the whole structure. Bebop resembles the contrapuntal music of the eighteenth century more than anything else, and the forms are surprisingly rigid.

In an attempt to break out of that rigidity, a number of talented players in the sixties began to experiment with new ways of making jazz. Improvisation based on altered scales, or modes, sometimes at several removes from the underlying harmony, was an early breakaway. Normal structures were interrupted for long sequences of free playing. Meter was no longer so strict. Changes no longer had to be stated so explicitly as before—there were other ways of playing together and knowing where you were in a given tune.

It was a time of enthusiasm for the new. Ornette Coleman. Cecil Taylor. As a result, Jarrett rapidly attracted the attention of a small, sophisticated audience. He went through various phases, including what he calls a "linear period" when he rarely played even the simplest chords but concentrated on blindingly fast lines, and his audience understood. When he moved on, they understood that, too.

The major vehicle for his jazz work was a group composed of himself, the modern bassist Charlie Haden and Paul Motian, who had played drums with Bill Evans, one of the masters of the post-bop era. Working with his own tunes and his own forms, Jarrett explored improvisation, group improvisation, straight-ahead playing, free playing, sound effects, exotic rhythms—every sort of jazz with the possible exception of ballads, in which he seems not to have been particularly interested. The emphasis was on the act of playing rather than on the presentation of material. His passionate improvisations and his sensational technique began to attract attention. The group, to which eventually Dewey Redman was added on saxophone, electrified audiences in both the United States and Europe, even audiences unfamiliar with avant-garde jazz, through the sheer force and energy of the music. Jarrett played with them, off and on, for more than ten years.

He also worked as a sideman with Charles Lloyd, the saxophonist, and for more than a year with Miles Davis—a post that in certain circles meant you had definitely arrived. Jarrett's rise was not swift, but it was steady, and his musical growth was tangible. (A comparison of *Gary Burton / Keith Jarrett* [Atlantic, 1971] with *Keith Jarrett / Shades* [Impulse, 1976] shows how much he improved in five years.) By the early 1970s, he was a highly respected jazz player.

But he did not stop there. Jarrett began a series of solo piano recitals in Europe, playing his own tunes at first, then including long sections of two-handed improvisation. There were at least two reasons for the standing-room-only audiences his concerts soon were attracting. First, the music, which existed somewhere between jazz and (for want of a better term) serious music, drew devotees of both. Second, Jarrett is a performer of almost hypnotic power. Whatever else it is, a piano recital is a theatrical event, and European audiences have always been responsive to that aspect of concerts. The elegant, romantic figure of Franz Liszt once held the entire continent in thrall. Liszt would remove his white gloves, finger by finger, as he stood onstage before a concert, and fling them to the wives and daughters of the bourgeoisie gathered under the footlights like so many groupies. Jarrett is much too serious to engage in that sort of foolishness, but he is a dramatic player nonetheless — singing as he plays, or rising from the bench to stab at the keys, or suddenly giving voice to a great whooping shout as he discovers something. His physical involvement in the act of playing is unabashed and completely sincere — he would seem, at times, to be a dancer at the keyboard.

Gradually Jarrett dropped even the framework of his tunes as the basis for his concert work. He began to do pure improvisation, or something very close to it.

Strictly speaking, pure improvisation is an impossibility. There are always certain habits and mannerisms (he likes a four-note gliss of halftones, for example: F, F#, G, G#) and unconscious repetitions. Bad improvisers simply string discrete chunks of material together in different series, rearranging the order, but an ambitious player will try to free himself of his favorite licks and become purer. In this regard, Jarrett makes great demands on himself. He is able to improvise the way he does only because he has been playing the piano for so long, and such diverse music, that his hands can almost automatically sculpt out of the keyboard something close to what he hears in his inner ear. His hands, in a sense, contain *in themselves* the laws of harmony, cycles and mathematical relationships that make up Western music, without his brain being immediately involved. There is a special kind of biofeedback, a brain-hand loop, involved when Jarrett plays, and the signals are complicated.

The European connection led to Manfred Eicher, the German founder, producer and president of ECM Records. Jarrett's professional association and friendship with Eicher has had a profound effect on the course of his career. Not only was Eicher willing and eager to record the concert work and pay splendid royalties on the sales of the albums, but he also brought special technical skills to bear in making the records themselves. For the first time in his life, Jarrett was being recorded by people as dedicated as himself. When he found out Jarrett had written music for strings and piano, Eicher advanced the money to hire the musicians to play it, and eventually to record it. A courageous and significant decision, because, as it turned out, Jarrett's string music was better than anyone had any reason to anticipate.

(I should interrupt here to explain that when I first saw Jarrett perform in Carnegie Hall, with a large string section, playing a rather long piece of his own composition, I was so impressed by the clean, beautifully balanced, subtly voiced string writing that I confess I didn't think he had done it. I thought he'd written out some themes and given it to an orchestral arranger. I could not have been more wrong.)

Jarrett had no training in orchestration and little experience in hearing his written music actually played by anybody, and yet his natural talent, his musicality, his taste and, above all, his ear prevailed. "If I can hear it," he was to tell me, "it ought to work when I write it out." Given the almost ideal arrangement with Eicher, Jarrett has disbanded his group and moved away from jazz toward solo concerts and the writing of modern music. That is his path.

Jarrett occupies interesting territory. The energies of jazz and rock infuse his improvisations without limiting the forms he chooses to explore. His ensemble writing will undoubtedly become more ambitious as he gets the chance to hear it all performed. Most serious music in this country is written by academics or by academically trained composers who focus on certain prestigious competitions and, perforce, on the tastes and prejudices of the judges. It is, sad to say, often a nasty atmosphere, full of snobbism and contempt for the general audience, and it is no surprise that most of the music is thin stuff. Jarrett is free of all that nonsense. Whatever one thinks of his music, it comes from his heart. Classical music critics can, in confusion, call him naive, whatever that means, and jazz critics can call him cerebral, which is dead wrong, but the indications are that if anyone is going to write important music in America in the next twenty or thirty years it will be a nonacademic — someone like Keith Jarrett.

It isn't easy to see Jarrett. He is a private man, and he deals with the media reluctantly. It took five months to get his phone number. When I finally reached him, he spoke rapidly and to the point: I should send him some of my work and call back in a week. I mailed a short piece on Thelonious Monk, an article on the Rolling Stones and *Stop-Time*. During the second phone call I assured him that I did not use a notebook or a tape recorder. I wanted rather to meet him and spend some time with him, and see what happened. He agreed to see me, but would not commit himself to any specific period of time.

Eventually I arrived at a very small town in central New Jersey. Following instructions, I called Keith from the phone booth in front of the general store. "I can only give you a couple of hours," he said. "I'll come get you."

He arrived in a four-wheel-drive Ford Bronco and looked at my rented car. "Does it have snow tires?" It did not, and so we went in the Bronco. The last few hundred yards were along a narrow, snow-packed track through the woods. Jarrett's home, a refurbished farmhouse, sits on a steep incline, isolated from the outside world.

Inside, I met his wife, Margot, and his young son, Gabriel. We all sat on the floor in the living room and tried to assemble the various tubes of a new vacuum cleaner, without success. Margot and the boy disappeared into another part of the house. Once again, I was struck by the aura of energy that surrounds Jarrett. He spoke calmly and with few unnecessary words, yet there was a feeling of electric tension. I asked how he had come to live there.

"The city became impossible," he said. "When Margot and I first got there, we lived in the middle of Spanish Harlem. It was all we could afford, and it was a nightmare. I felt no connection to any of it." He stared at the floor. "We were kids then. We didn't know anything. Then we lived in Greenwich Village, in an apartment we couldn't afford, and that didn't work either. So we started looking around in the country and found this. A Guggenheim helped with the money part."

I asked him if he went to the city often—a drive of an hour and a half.

"Not much." (Later, Margot was to tell me, it felt as if they had spent more time in Europe than in New York.)

We talked in a general way about music, and I got the feeling Jarrett listens more to music of the past than to that of his own time. He became most animated talking about Handel, for instance. "Handel is underrated," he said firmly. "Listen to Handel side by side with Bach sometime. They complement one another. There's a clarity in Handel's music—a clarity." Jarrett does not vacillate—when he has an opinion he expresses it forcefully, so much so, in fact, that he sometimes sounds a bit defensive. At the very least, one notices in him a young man's tendency to have a firm position on almost every subject. His quickness of mind and the clean, focused language with which he expresses himself, without a trace of jargon, redeem him. Also, he doesn't push. His opinions are his own, and he does not proselytize.

"Stay for dinner," he said after a couple of hours. "There's plenty of food."

I accepted. Gabriel brought up drinks from the kitchen.

"What are we eating?" Jarrett asked the boy.

"Lamb leg," Gabe said. At the age of five, Gabriel is remarkably self-possessed. An only child, he knows how to get along with adults. Throughout my visit—which turned out to be two days—he remained cheerful, even-tempered, affectionate and busy. He addresses his parents by their first names.

In response to some gentle prodding from me, Jarrett rapidly described the outlines of his career, but it was clear that he wasn't much interested in pursuing his own history. He becomes slightly impatient when talking about the past, as if dwelling on it will distract attention from the present.

The question of strength came up—personal strength. Jarrett seems to have always remained true to his inner vision. Over a period of many years, he has not compromised. I told him I was curious about the source of that strength, and I asked him if he was a religious man. The question caught him off guard; he didn't answer immediately.

"A lot of young players seem to be into something," I said.

Jarrett got up and went into the kitchen. He needed to collect his thoughts, or so it seemed to me.

When he returned he said, "Some of them are trying to iden- tify with their audience, with the different fads, and some of them are just gullible. The trouble is, it's hard to talk about these things seriously now, because the coin has been debased. I can tell you that I'm on a path—Margot and I have been on a path for the last twelve years, and what started it off was a book I read, but I'd rather not get into it."

I asked if he had had a guide or a teacher.

"No. I did it myself, with books. It changed my life, and that was long before people started getting involved with this sort of thing. I got in the habit of not talking about it, because people would have thought I was crazy, in those days." He paused. "There's no point anyway. It's not about talking, it's about being."

I asked him what the book was.

"Never mind," he said. "It was just a book. Another culture, another time—but the things he said made sense."

Dinner at the Jarretts' was somewhat more formal than one might expect of a young American couple. Served in the dining room, with place settings and candles. Lamb, an eggplant casse- role and a very good bottle of wine. Keith obviously enjoys eat- ing—he had second helpings of everything. Margot is an alert woman, with an air of competence and, at the same time, a slightly abstracted nervousness. She is pretty, bright and per- haps a bit more fun-loving than her husband, but she contains herself in deference to him. They met in Allentown, and they have the closeness of people who have grown up together.

The talk veered to the subject of Miles Davis, with whom Jarrett had a good relationship. Suddenly, from the end of the table, young Gabriel piped up. "Is this still the interview?" he asked. The boy was used to more attention at the table. His tone made it clear that he didn't resent the lack of it, he just wanted to get things straight.

"No," I said. "I'm just talking now."

"Okay." He nodded and ate a piece of lamb.

After dinner, everyone helped clear the table.

"I want you to hear something," Jarrett said, leading me through the living room into the study. "I did some concerts in Japan a couple of months ago, and I just got the tapes." A large desk, a couch facing a pair of speakers and a wall of books and records. The library was that of a man who reads for information rather than for fun. I noticed some Ouspensky, some Gurdjieff and a book on Islam—presumably, Jarrett also reads for enlightenment. He poured a brandy for me, and then a small one for himself, and put on the tape.

"These were odd concerts in one way," he said. "I usually know while I'm playing how good it is, or if it's horrible, but I didn't in Japan. There was a lot of strange stuff going on in my head. I'd get off the stage without really knowing. And depressed sometimes, which is *very* unusual for me after a concert. But Manfred knew it was good, and so did Margot, and those are the two people I trust most about music. It turned out they were right. It's going to be an eight-record album. Eight records!"

The tape began, piano notes dropping like pearls. Instantly Jarrett was transformed, entirely focused on the music. I thought I could sense an attempt on his part to remain still, but it was clearly impossible for him. When he listens, he is swept away, and it is a sort of muted version of what happens to him when he plays. After every phrase he gives a sharp, reflexive exhalation of breath, as if he has lived through that phrase in the act of listening to it—a kind of tight laugh, vaguely reminiscent of the short, sniffing sound a boxer makes as he throws a punch. The music, the phrases, are like breathing to him. When the lines get long he rocks back and forth, and dips his head, and then raises it as the line soars. The gestures are pressurized and mysteriously eloquent. It is as if he is straining physically to become the music, to turn his body into sound.

On first hearing, the Japanese concerts were very good indeed. The level of improvisation seemed higher than the German concerts—more complicated structures and less reliance on repetitive figures in the left hand (although they still remain to some extent). Some sequences were so daring, so beautifully developed, that I had to remind myself it was improvisation.

"What does it feel like when you're doing it?" I asked. "Does it feel as free as it sounds?"

"Yes," he said without hesitation.

At one point, as he changed tapes, I said that I'd always been impressed by his touch and his ability to make the piano sing.

"An interviewer once asked me what pianists I particularly admired, and I said Rubinstein. It turned out Rubinstein was being interviewed for some Swiss newspaper at the same time, and they asked him who were the promising young pianists, and he mentioned me. I've never met him, of course. I had no idea he'd ever even heard me."

We listened until past midnight. Part of the time, Margot joined us, and when she was there Jarrett never took his eyes off her, watching her reaction to the music, some of which she hadn't heard since it was played in concert in Japan.

I spent the night in the guest room. Margot's loom was set up in one corner, surrounded by piles of brightly colored wool. I thought about the last thing Jarrett had told me, when I'd asked about his immediate plans. He would be writing, he'd said. Deutsche Grammophon had commissioned him to compose a piece for the Boston Symphony, to be conducted by Seiji Ozawa, with himself playing piano. "My God," I'd said. "That's wonderful. I'll be there. I'll fly over from Nantucket." For the first time, I'd heard a note of doubt in Jarrett's voice—very faint, to be sure, because it was said lightly: "If I finish it."

At breakfast, I asked him if, in view of the direction his career was taking, he was finished playing jazz.

"I don't like to rule anything out," he said, "but I'm not forming a new group, if that's what you mean."

We spent the morning listening to some jazz, and a new album of Keith improvising on a Baroque organ in a monastary in Germany. (He discovered a way to get quartertones by pulling the stops partway.) Jarrett was eager to have me try his Steinway B grand, a recent acquisition, which I did, feeling more than a little self-conscious. "Don't worry," he said, "I won't say anything." He stood behind me while I played. When I was finished he said, "It's nice in here, don't you think," striking some keys about two octaves above middle C. "It's very strong along in here."

I made my goodbyes to Margot and Gabe, and Keith offered to drive me back to my car. As we walked across the driveway, he pointed up the hill to a small barn. "I'll be up there for a while now. There's nothing in it except a fireplace, a lamp, a drafting table and a stack of music paper." We got in the car. "So far I've got twenty-six pages of percussion," he said, shifting gears. "Some very soft parts. It's hard to play softly, you know." I suddenly had a fantasy of being Keith Jarrett and walking into Symphony Hall in Boston and hearing the orchestra play my music. I said it seemed to me that that must be an almost unimaginably gratifying experience.

"Yes. That's the reward," he said. "After all the pain of doing it, you just give it away. You just turn it over, and it isn't yours anymore." He smiled. "But then you get to hear it."

1977

(A note from now. The Boston Symphony had a great deal of trouble with Jarrett's piece and never performed it. As far as I know, it has never been played by anyone, which seems to be Jarrett's wish.)

Marsalis at Twenty-three

I T's CROWDED in the shallow lobby of Carnegie Hall. People are lined up twenty deep at the ticket windows; others rush up the steps from Fifty-seventh Street, mill around, dart back and forth. Wynton Marsalis stands near the central door. He wears a long, black semiformal topcoat. As he moves his head the light flashes off the gold bridge of his circular eyeglasses. I can see the tickets in his hand.

We climb to the first balcony and take our seats. It looks like a full house, and Marsalis is pleased. We've come to see Maurice André, the French trumpet and cornet virtuoso, perform with the Houston Symphony Orchestra. André is an important figure to Marsalis, not least because André has described him as "potentially the greatest trumpeter of all time." Wynton leans forward as André—a rotund, vaguely unkempt, gray-haired man—comes onstage. The orchestra begins Hummel's late-eighteenth-century Trumpet Concerto. As André stands with his horn at the ready, waiting for his entrance, Marsalis whispers, "Imagine all the stuff going through his mind right now."

Indeed, there is tension in the air. Not just because the soloist is about to begin, but because of properties inherent in the instrument he will play. The trumpet is a difficult instrument: easy enough to play badly, simply making approximate notes over a couple of octaves, with occasional vibrato, as in a marching band; but to play well, to control the shape and timbre of the tone, to control the dynamics, to play on pitch, to control the beginning and end of each note and especially to use the full range of the instrument—all this is very difficult. Every instrument becomes harder to play as the player attempts to extend his control, but with the trumpet it happens early on. At any moment even an experienced player can purse his lips, depress a valve, blow and get a split tone, or no tone at all, an empty hiss of air as if from a deflating inner tube. Moisture condenses, valves stick or leak, tuning slides don't slide—things can go wrong. And should any of these mishaps occur during a performance, there is no place to hide. The sound a trumpet makes is, by its nature, totally up front, totally exposed. It is not an instrument for the faint-hearted.

André plays the Hummel smoothly. Marsalis knows every note, having recorded the piece himself for Columbia Records, and makes small, crisp gestures in the air with his hands at the tempo changes. His pleasure in the music is obvious. At the end of the last movement he stands to applaud. André leaves the stage.

We listen to a symphony by Paul Cooper, a contemporary American composer. Marsalis is attentive but not involved. "Sad stuff," he says. "Why doesn't he use rhythm? Look at all those guys in the timpani just standing around." He goes on to point out that one of the strengths of Baroque music is the fact that it swings.

André returns to play Albinoni's Trumpet Concerto in D minor. "This piece is hard, man," Marsalis says. "It's a bitch." But André seems in even better form than before and handles the most difficult passages with verve. Somewhere in the middle of the adagio section Marsalis whispers in my ear. "In here's when you start getting tired. All those long notes." But if André is tired, I can't hear it. He finishes to strong applause. "Maurice." Marsalis shakes his head in admiration. "Old Maurice."

The audience calls André back from the wings several times, and finally he brings out his cornet and the hall falls still. "Music," he calls out in a thick French accent, "from the French Renaissance." He raises the instrument to his lips, plays a few bars, and suddenly a note splits and he stops. The horn has failed, presumably. Flustered, he dashes offstage for a substitute, comes back and plays his short encore.

During intermission, the assistant manager of the hall had found us in our seats and informed Marsalis that André was aware that he was in the audience, and that if Marsalis would like to go backstage after the concert, the assistant manager would be pleased to escort us. We move now through various side halls, down stairs, through doors, up steps, and emerge in the wings. Marsalis is recognized by various members of the Houston Symphony, who offer compliments on his recent Grammy Awards (Best Classical Recording and Best Jazz Recording in the same year—a first), and by several other people who ask for his autograph, which he cheerfully gives. When he breaks free, he asks a member of the brass section just coming offstage where David is. Marsalis went to the Juilliard School with David, a tuba player. ("Him and me," Marsalis will say, "were always the last ones in the practice room. One A.M., man, we in there playing.") David arrives, a hefty, rosy-cheeked young man, and breaks into a smile. They fall on each other, pound each other's backs, laugh and talk for a while. But the assistant manager attends. "Wynton," David says in parting, "keep doing what you're doing." His tone is serious now. "It's beautiful. Keep on."

The soloist's dressing room is crowded. Some speak French and some English. André greets Marsalis with open arms and a flood of French, none of which Marsalis understands except the intent. "Tell him," Marsalis begins, and I am kept busy translating: The question of the horn that failed during the encore. (A bad valve.) Marsalis's debt to André with regard to learning how to approach Albinoni. André's admiration for Marsalis's Haydn recording. Some photographers move in and take pictures of the two men. The maestros are in a good mood and do not mind holding one of André's trumpets between them. Strobes flash.

Before he leaves, Marsalis makes a point of saying a word or two to the members of the Houston brass section. Signing autographs all the way, he finds them here and there in the crowd. He compliments the first trumpet, touching his arm in a fraternal gesture. Even as he gives compliments, he is receiving them. Musicians and music lovers shout encouragement to him from hallways and doorways, from the backstage stairs as he passes by. He gives a last few autographs at the rear door and accepts an open invitation from the assistant manager to attend any concert at any time as a guest of the house, and we push through and are out on the street. Marsalis strides along at a brisk clip. "I'm hungry," he says. "Let's go someplace and eat." He is twenty-three years old.

In the cab going uptown we begin to talk jazz—a fast exchange of names, important recordings, influences, hip bebop lines (Wynton is an excellent scat singer), little-known players and so on. In an informal setting Marsalis speaks a rich polyglot. Like many other young black artists and intellectuals, he mixes into his commentary street slang, hip argot, ordinary American, professional vernacular, southern expressions, urban parlance and whatever else he needs. His speech is unselfconscious, spontaneous, quick, intelligent and virtually impossible to re-create on the page.

In the restaurant Wynton orders fried squid with hot sauce, Dover sole and a glass of orange juice. His taste for seafood is perhaps related to his childhood in New Orleans. (Ellis Marsalis, Wynton's father, is one of the best jazz pianists in Louisiana.) He relates his past perfunctorily, as if aware that it might be of interest to others but isn't to him.

His father was clever, he says, and simply left the best jazz records around the house for him and his brothers to play or not. He didn't push. Wynton began serious study of the trumpet at the age of twelve. His high school teacher was an important influence. He learned to practice and apply himself. "The brothers be out on the street, man. Standing around being cool. Into it. Like, 'We cool, we heavy dudes. Let's go burn a house. Let's go rape somebody.' Incredibly stupid shit, man. I say no, and go off and practice."

During high school he joined a band with his older brother Branford, a fine, solid saxophone player, and played funk or jazz or whatever was necessary to get gigs. At fourteen, he performed the Haydn Trumpet Concerto with the New Orleans Philharmonic; at sixteen, the Brandenburg Concerto No. 2 in F Major. From the start, he wanted to play both classical and jazz. (Real jazz, which is to say modern jazz from bebop roots, was an art music—his father's domain—an adult music for an adult audience, to be approached carefully.) Practice paid off. By the age of seventeen Wynton had developed remarkable technical proficiency and was rewarded with several scholarships, first to the Tanglewood Music Center and then to Juilliard.

He orders another orange juice. "I didn't know much about Juilliard. I just wanted to get to New York." He left home and began to study music—both classical and jazz—while continuing to practice his instrument. He worked hard. His roommate for a while was the percussionist Akira Tana, and in this Marsalis was lucky. Tana is older, knowledgeable in both genres, cultured, even-tempered and intellectually generous—a perfect counterpoint to the raw, passionate, opinionated Marsalis. In bull sessions that went on till all hours of the night Tana would attempt to deal with Marsalis's anger at what he thought was happening to jazz, his anger at looking for heroes and not finding them.

Here in the restaurant, five years later, it is clear that Marsalis continues to feel strongly about the sad trend in the seventies and eighties of great jazz players chasing larger and younger audiences.

"It's upside down," he says. "It's backwards. They're pandering to a bunch of kids. Listen, when I'm forty-five years old, why the hell should I pay attention to a bunch of kids? Who just want party music! What am I going to learn? The kids should be learning from the older cats, right?"

For Marsalis, jazz is art, and art is to be revered and protected, and artists are duty-bound to meet the challenge. To do otherwise is to cop out, to be sucked down into the purgatory of mass taste. It's a familiar position, a cliché even, but Marsalis doesn't care. He means it.

At the Grammy Awards Wynton played the Hummel, which has gained him an international reputation, and a demanding jazz tune. He made a few brief remarks indicating his belief that jazz is music with great traditions and sort of built-in safeguards against commercialism and bad taste. To some this smacked of elitism. It also suggested that although the music was protected, musicians were not. On the same program Quincy Jones, who was once an important force in jazz, and of whom much was once expected, accepted several awards for his work producing for Michael Jackson. Herbie Hancock—one of the best jazz pianists of his generation—pranced around the stage in a glitzy rock-star outfit, a strange electric-guitar-cum-mini-piano hanging around his neck, playing the funk music for which he and his group had won an award. "I'm prouder of this award than anything that's happened to me in twenty-five years in the business," he said. If Marsalis did not respect these older jazzmen, he would not be angry with them. Indeed, his anger is a function of his respect.

"Listen," he says, "I've got every record Miles Davis ever made. I know what Miles did, how great he was. But then, man . . ." He shakes his head. "He wanted the kids, and he came down to all that electric shit."

Marsalis knows there are people around who don't like to hear a young player talk this way. One hears the following kind of argument: Columbia Records picked Marsalis for a major push and made a large investment in him at the expense of other young talent. Marsalis achieved financial security almost immediately and remains insensitive to the financial pressures experienced by everyone else, particularly the great players of the generation before him. The charge is made that he has not paid his dues. Especially in black jazz circles, connections are drawn between the purity of a man's music and the degree of pain he has experienced. Marsalis can answer that it was not all peaches and cream at Columbia, that they signed him to play funk and he had to fight every step of the way to be allowed to play jazz, let alone classical. Before he became a great success, a single individual within the company had supported him, and everyone else had been indifferent, according to Marsalis. As for dues, he feels he paid significantly in the practice room for half his lifetime, and if he can now make a living with his horn, so much the better.

"I listen to funk sometimes," he says. "It's fun, sometimes. Hell, I listen to Michael Jackson, sometimes." He smiles. For a moment he is young, making a confession, as a young man might admit to a holdover fondness for a nice bowl of Count Chocula in the morning. "I listen to rock, but it's hard to watch most of it." He leans forward, serious again. "They confuse emoting with emotion." He orders yet another orange juice.

"Hey, you remember that Clifford Brown line? Talk about emotion." He grabs my wrist and begins to sing scat.

Marsalis has bought a small nineteenth-century townhouse in a mixed middle-class neighborhood in Brooklyn near the Manhattan Bridge. His brother Branford lives in the apartment above his own. Sunday morning he answers the door and I go inside. "No furniture yet," he explains. "They just finished the remodeling." The front room has a mattress on the floor, a single folding chair and a tape player. A brand-new Yamaha baby grand piano occupies the next room, with stacks of music here and there, half a drum set piled against the wall. In the back there is an open area with tall windows looking out on some trees, and a tiny kitchen off to the side. Marsalis is dressed in Adidas sneakers, running pants and a T-shirt. He has made himself a breakfast of English muffins, eggs and cheese. He looks mournfully into the frying pan. "I messed this up. Didn't do it right." But he eats with relish, standing up. "I moved five times since I came to New York. Started uptown and worked my way down." It is an elegant space, everything in scale, lots of light, shiny wood floors. A dream pad, I can't help thinking, for a single young man—and yet sensible also in terms of size, upkeep and the lack of any neighbor on the other side of the wall, since the house is at the end of its block. Trumpet players have to worry about neighbors.

Marsalis goes into the kitchen, and I sit down at the piano and start fooling around. He emerges after a few minutes, smiling. "Sounds good. Those elevenths are hip." He sits next to me on the bench and plays bass lines while I run through the blues. Immediately there is a sense of energy, of energy propelling his notes.

"Let me show you some stuff," he says, and I move to the end

of the bench to give him room. "My tunes, some stuff I'm working on." Wynton is not a performance pianist, but he can play
more than well enough to explicate, as it were, the music he has
written for jazz quintet. He plays with concentration, making
sure to get the voicings right. "Now, in here, *ping!* That's a harmonic for the bass player. See? *Ping.* Right there."

His chords have a modern sound, but even more modern is
their movement. He gets patterns going that resolve in unex-
pected and yet perfectly logical places. His harmonics are sophisticated, and I ask him if he learned the mathematical part at
Juilliard. "Mostly in the practice room," he says. "In there with
tapes of Miles, Trane, all the different groups. I just worked out
the chords, man. Play it over and over till I get it. You know, like
I hear something and think, 'What the hell is that?' and keep on
till I get it. Jazz is totally logical. Everything is connected."

"When you're writing a tune," I ask, "where do you start?
With the chords?"

"No, no. The lines. I hear the lines, and I don't worry about
the chords. They'll be there." He plays, and then the phone rings
and he gets up to answer it. I slide over and try to play some of
the chord patterns he's just shown me, without much success.
After a while I switch into the key of B-flat and start improvising on the old-fashioned changes of "I've Got Rhythm." Suddenly I hear Marsalis on the trumpet, getting louder as he
comes in from the other room, playing straight-ahead bebop in
the style, more or less, of Clifford Brown. Marsalis is goofing, to
be sure, but it's dazzling. He moves from eighth-note lines to
sixteenth-note lines (twice as fast) without effort, making elegant constructions chorus by chorus. And no matter what the
speed, all the notes are fully formed and exactly on pitch.

We jam for half an hour, play a Monk ballad, but my heart
isn't in it. I feel like a child who has the skills to ride a pony but
has been mistakenly mounted on Man o' War. Once *he* starts,

Marsalis can't help himself—he moves from one level to the next because his improvisation leads him there, up to where the air is bracing and the light is pure. Since I can't follow, I wind up feeling as if I'm playing at the bottom of a swimming pool. We go back into the front room. He brings his horn.

"Don't mind if I walk around while we talk," he says. "I even practice like this." He moves back and forth across the gleaming floor while I sit on the folding chair. His body is compact, well proportioned and lithe. I notice for the first time how small his hands are. He is an attractive man—a round face, strong eyes, complexion somewhere between cinnamon and café au lait. He seems to radiate healthiness and a sense of relish toward life in general. He's a bit speedy, but it feels natural, not at all manic—a controlled exhilaration.

We talk, and he plays bits of music every now and then. Fats Navarro. His fingers fly over the valves. "Miles got a lot from Navarro," he says. "This is Pops" (Louis Armstrong)—he does a couple of figures. "Pops was the best ever, you know. Absolutely the best." As we talk about other trumpet players it occurs to me that Marsalis has the perfect personality for the instrument—self-confident, open, trusting, appropriately aggressive and warm. Miles Davis was the greatest player of the fifties, sixties and, by default, the seventies, and his contribution involves much more than simply playing the trumpet; but at the same time his minimalism, his tendency to avoid all but the middle register, his short solos and famous habit (for more than twenty years) of turning his back to the audience, his coolness, his shyness—all seem to suggest a personality imperfectly suited for the horn. Marsalis has a long way to go in jazz before reaching the artistic level of Davis, but somehow he seems more of a trumpet player. He wants to take on the whole instrument, its entire range, discover everything it can do and apply it to both jazz and classical.

"Jazz is harder," Marsalis says. "You don't know what you're going to have to do ten bars after whatever it is you're doing." High jazz improvisation demands much more than technique. "My problem is sometimes I'll just be playing." He stops and looks over to make sure I've understood. "I get excited, and I'll just be playing." He twiddles the middle fingers of his right hand in a gesture to dramatize emptiness. "Most people can't hear it. They like velocity. They like it to be flashy."

I ask him if adverse criticism hurts.

"No, it's cool," he says. "Cats hear me, they say, 'Oh, he got that from Brownie,' or, 'He's trying to sound like Miles, or Dizzy, or whatever.'" He looks at his horn. "I'm not trying to sound like anybody, man. I'm trying to sound like me."

Without taking anything away from his extraordinary musical and technical achievements, it was inevitable that someone like Marsalis would emerge. Miles Davis's cool romanticism had its run, and Marsalis's hot classicism means a return to the full use of the trumpet in jazz and perhaps even a challenge to the saxophone, which has been the dominant instrument since Charlie Parker. What could not have been anticipated is the extent to which his jazz experience has prepared him for a fresh interpretation of the classical repertoire. At the age of twenty-three, Marsalis is a complete musician, eager to press forward in both traditions. He represents a new generation of American players who are reviving jazz after more than a decade of somnolence.

In his jazz records so far, Marsalis has not seemed to be reaching for an easily recognizable personal style, as did Maynard Ferguson, Chet Baker, Miles Davis, Chuck Mangione and others. Instead, he seems to draw from everywhere and continue to expand; his style will emerge fully only when *he* has reached the limits of the instrument. For some listeners, that is a large part of the excitement about Wynton Marsalis. "Everybody should just leave him alone and let him get there," says A. B. Spellman, the jazz historian. "He's the best thing that's happened in a long, long time."

Marsalis left Juilliard to play with Art Blakey's Jazz Messengers, a quintet that produced many of the most important trumpeters of the past twenty-five years. After that, in the summer of 1981 he went on the road with Herbie Hancock, Ron Carter and Tony Williams (Miles Davis's old rhythm section). "I learned from everybody," Marsalis says. "Particularly Blakey. When I started with him, I didn't even know how to play a ballad."

He lifts the horn and begins to play a Baroque cadenza, very rapidly alternating phrases in the high register with a sort of figured bass in the low register. "Can you dig it? Sounds like two horns."

I ask him if he thinks he will be able to continue to play both classical and jazz as a professional or whether he'll eventually have to concentrate on one or the other.

"I want to do both," he says. "In jazz, there's stuff I want to explore. You know, people solo with a four-bar feel, or eight-bar. They been doing that. I want to break out—go over bar lines, make the structures different." He holds up his free hand. "But always respect the form." He ambles away. "Pops went over bar lines. You can hear him solo sometimes, he's just not worried at all about bar lines. And the form is always there underneath." The doorbell rings. "Stuff I want to do with meter. I got a blues, the first eight bars are in four, and the last four bars are in three and a half, man." He slips out to answer the door and returns with a strikingly pretty young woman. He makes the introductions and goes off to take a shower. When he comes back, in a jacket and slacks, he asks, "How do I look? Is it all right?"

• • •

Three weeks later, a jazz concert at the McCarter Theatre in Princeton, New Jersey. The event is sold out—an elite audience of intellectuals, academics, music lovers, students and local notables. Marsalis, Branford and their rhythm section come onstage. "Thanks for coming out to hear live jazz," Marsalis says. The quintet launches into an advanced, high-energy set. The music is fast and complicated, making demands on the audience. Marsalis's tunes are full of alternating time signatures, floating tonalities and sophisticated structural devices. They are also elegant, witty, emotional, crisp ensemble pieces in which balance is preserved, the sound of the quintet predominant over any individual instrument. His own solos have an ebullient celebratory quality as he builds lines, pops into related scales and surprises us with sudden silences. He brings all sorts of instrumental effects to bear in what seems a thoroughly natural way—smears, growls, color effects, partial valve effects—never for their own sake, but to get deeper into the solo. If the audience does not fully understand the music—a brilliant modern extrapolation of the fifties and sixties classic bebop quintet sound of Art Blakey, Horace Silver and others—they are nevertheless aware of the skill with which it is being played. The first set ends, a polished statement of Marsalis's sense of new jazz emerging from what has come before.

Backstage, Marsalis is in good humor. Someone remarks that the drummer might have overplayed somewhat; having begun the set at such a high pitch, he had nowhere to go. "That's true," Marsalis says, and then he laughs, "but he sure played some mean stuff. Whew!" He wipes his brow with a handkerchief. "Anyway, change of pace next set." He walks around in the wings, saying hello to friends who have come backstage, sharing a joke with his road manager, shaking hands with two teenage fans. "Practice," Marsalis says to the boys as they move away.

The second set is generous, offering some familiar ballads

and a couple of medium-tempo tunes. The audience seems to melt. The ballads are warm and tastefully wrought, full of intelligent emotion, and the tunes swing nicely. At the end, an ovation from the audience, who won't sit down until they get an encore. The quintet plays a light riff with some delightful, dryly funny variations—an almost ironic coda, a satire on technique—and the concert is over.

High spirits backstage. The concert has gone well—it had a shape, and the shape worked. Individually, each player seems pleased with his own playing, but there is also a collective sense of pride in having presented jazz well to a potentially difficult audience.

Branford has to leave quickly. He's already late for a gig in New York. "Be careful," somebody says. "Remember Clifford." Branford acknowledges the warning. (Clifford Brown died in a car crash on the New Jersey Turnpike. A number of jazzmen have died on that road over the years.) These are young men who take care of themselves.

Wynton thanks his booking agent, shakes hands with dozens of well-wishers, signs some programs, then breaks away and steers me to a corner.

"I've got the summer circuit and then the trip to Japan," he says, "but then you've got to come hear the new stuff, with the new band." He gestures toward the rhythm section across the room. "We've been together years now, and it's time for a shift. I've got this bass player, cat is sixteen years old, and I'm telling you, you won't believe it. He is completely open. Tell him to play six bars in four and then two bars in seven, he just goes ahead and does it. I mean, he's so young he doesn't have any shit to unlearn, you know? We're going to play jazz you won't believe." He smiles. "Really."

1984

Marsalis at Thirty-four

IN THE OLD Masonic Hall being used as a recording studio, Wynton Marsalis tells the band to take a ten-minute break, steps down from the podium, comes over and gives me a hug. We sit down in the old theater seats.

"Man," he says, "I am *tired* of all this stuff they're writing about me. It has nothing do with the music."

"The dogs bark, but the caravan rolls on," I quote.

He laughs. "Hey, that's good. I'll have to remember that."

I had read various sniping reports in the media. That he was an archivist, insufficiently avant-garde. That he didn't hire enough white players or play enough music written by whites. That he was provincial. That he wasn't sensitive enough to multiculturalism (translation: not part of the current fad of "world music," whatever that is). Low-level cavils from the right and from the left, which had saddened me, since Marsalis is a musical genius, the leader of a powerful renaissance in jazz and a tireless educator of the young. Personally, he is charismatic, a lover of argument, a firm, not to say tenacious, defender of his opinions about music, politics, philosophy and everything else, very bright and mildly impatient—all of which rubs some people the wrong way.

As both an artist and an observer of the musical scene, Marsalis is drawn to clarity. He abhors confusion. Unfortunately, a good deal of confusion continues to exist in the jazz world, partly because the old order is giving way to the new and partly because of the history of obscurantism, defensiveness and hermeticism that has prevailed for something like fifty years. Jazz is a fine art, the only fine art to have been developed from scratch in America, where recognition, paradoxically, has been slow in coming—perhaps because the music emerged from black culture, from the bottom (economically speaking) up. Some protectiveness and secrecy on the part of the musicians were perhaps to be expected. Many black musicians were covetous, and some grew angry through the years as they saw white players making more money than themselves playing jazz or watered-down jazz. (It used to be said that jazz players were black, Jewish, Italian or Irish—very close to the truth—and it was the blacks getting the short end of the stick from the union, the recording studios and the bookers.)

As well, jazz had an ominous side. Most players were honest, hard-working men, often subsidizing their music with ordinary jobs, known as day gigs, but there were also drug addicts and dealers, thieves and pimps. A number of famous players in the 1940s and 1950s ran strings of prostitutes to augment their incomes. Thus there were people creating sublimely beautiful music while living sublimely ugly lives (strengthening the vulgar and false idea that the authenticity of the music was a function of the degree of misery in the life of the player). Public perception of jazz has been heavily tainted with notions of criminality and degeneracy, and lingers still, albeit faintly, despite the fact that conditions have changed completely.

There are jazz programs in virtually all the colleges and universities. Jazz clubs around the country are "high class" and expensive. Institutional efforts like Jazz at Lincoln Center (of which Marsalis is the artistic director, thus drawing heat from

people who would like a different kind of programming) are
springing up in major cities. The new generation of players are
by and large educated, cultured people in their twenties, more
likely to be vegetarians than drug addicts, more likely to run
three miles a day than smoke cigarettes, more likely to be carry-
ing an organ-donor card than a gun. There is a French expression, *nostalgie de la boue,* which means nostalgia for the gutter,
and it is perhaps that preoccupation slowing down so many jazz
fans, observers and writers from recognizing reality.

Jazz is American. It belongs to everybody now, black, white,
Latin, to all those who have added to it and all those who have
been moved by it. Fresh breezes are invigorating the music,
which in turn promises once again to invigorate American culture itself. (And at this point, American culture needs all the
good stuff it can get.) Heretofore, composers working from the
European tradition have dipped in for a bit of spice and energy
—Ives, Copland, Gershwin and others who used jazzy effects—
but I believe the current renaissance will lead to a time when
jazz is no longer marginalized, when artists working in jazz traditions will create work as strong as, and perhaps stronger than,
the music that came out of the European tradition.

For a long time, jazz fans and players have been obsessed
with the idea of progress. Because of the speed and abruptness
of the bebop revolution, people were looking for something
quick, and what they got, mostly, were garden paths leading to
noplace in particular. Progress is a dubious concept in any art—
have we had progress in poetry, in the novel, in painting or in
dance? I don't think so.

The idea is inappropriately linear, less useful than the model
of a kind of pulsating spiral, moving out, moving in, but over
time growing larger, covering more territory. Jazz is at a point
when the spiral is moving out, and all the old arguments,

sports-fan mentalities, show-biz preoccupations and theoretical dogmas seem as dated as the novels of Mickey Spillane. It will take a new generation of writers to write about a new generation of players and composers, and let us hope that deconstructionists, politically correct busybodies and agenda-driven theorists will not be in their number.

For the moment, a distinction should be drawn between outdated notions of progress and modern attempts to trace and extend the organic evolution of jazz. (The basic concept from the old days of biology, that ontogeny recapitulates phylogeny—or, more simply stated, that individual growth mirrors the history of the species—is useful in music.) The way to strengthen one's ability to tell the difference between progress and evolution is to study the canon—that music which has had the longest and deepest influence—because the canon contains the evolutionary signposts and implies how jazz can spiral outward without losing its identity.

For instance, the canon suggests an expansion into long forms, forms of a length we usually associate with so-called classical music. One of the missions of Jazz at Lincoln Center is to lay down a foundation for the future of jazz by presenting important works from the canon with all the passion and intelligence that can be brought to bear.

I remember sitting all night at a Manhattan club called the Half Note listening to John Coltrane play with his famous rhythm section. I was there for the first public performance of "My Favorite Things," a superficially sappy song sung by Julie Andrews in *The Sound of Music.* Coltrane stated the themes, instantly making it his own through his phrasing, and proceeded to improvise in an intricately structured series of related scales and modes more and more remote from the original.

He played for almost an hour, his slender soprano saxophone

heartbreakingly tender one moment, thick and angry the next, singing out cries, as it were, from many hearts. There was so much emotion, so much density of emotion, I was effectively hypnotized for the entire performance.

Later, as I thought about his ascent through the different scales and modes (over a kind of tonal drone from the other instruments), I thought I realized why he had picked that unlikely tune. It was harmonically perfect for a grand tour of related scales, with which he created what the great Nadia Boulanger used to call *la grande ligne,* a clear swooping line that arises in a piece from the beginning to the end. The inner music. Evolution.

I had never heard anything like it in jazz. To see and hear it right there in front of me, brand new, was more thrilling than I can describe. What I feel now, as I sense all of jazz on the brink of a new era, is the anticipation of the same kind of excitement.

After the ten-minute break, the recording session recommences. The piece, *Blood on the Fields,* is the largest and most daring of Marsalis's compositions to date, and the first to include voices.

I sit beside Eric Reed, a superb young pianist from Los Angeles who plays the very difficult score. Chords are not fully noted but suggested by the traditional jazz symbols, which means that Eric is free to voice them any way he wants. In order to get the best sound, he has to listen with extraordinary care to what all the other instruments are doing and decide his voicings on the spot. Sometimes the chords come four to the bar. His playing is simply dazzling.

During one sequence, he prepares the piano by placing his jacket over the treble strings, improvises a series of dancing staccato riffs, removes the jacket and plays the last chords of the section. In the small silence that follows, he turns his head to me. "'How High the Moon,'" he says, "it ain't." He speaks the truth. It's a new day for American music.

Jazz is a wonderfully open and elastic music that has, in its relatively short history, absorbed energy from myriad sources. Europe, Africa, Cuba and Latin America are where the harmonies, scales, rhythms and instruments came from. Jazz forms have emerged from gospel, marching-band music, Tin Pan Alley, rags, blues, show tunes, classical music, field hollers and so on—listed here in no special order.

A restless music, the best practitioners of which have adhered to Ezra Pound's credo, "Make it new," with particular intensity, sometimes to ill effect. As one might expect in such a volatile environment, there have been plenty of fads, panflashes, phony theories and dead ends.

The tension between the urge to make it new and the awareness of possible dead ends creates an atmosphere in which contention thrives. For more than forty years I've watched and listened as jazz people yelled, screamed, shook their fists and generally lost their cool over one issue after another. Obsessions with the idea of progress have obscured awareness of how jazz has moved through time, of what jazz carries from the past into the exigencies of the present and, indeed, what the music in fact is or should be.

Whatever he eventually came to believe, Louis Armstrong was initially deeply suspicious of bebop, which surfaced in Harlem in the late 1930s—an extremely important style whose harmonic complexity and contrapuntal sophistication created a new paradigm. Classical jazz, or Dixie, and modern jazz, or bebop, were to run in parallel paths, almost never touching, for more than fifty years. Only recently has jazz moved past this schism, because the young players see it all as related music, different colors on the same palette, all to be used.

Maybe the fighting started there, with the classical jazz / modern jazz split, but it grew to the point where it sometimes felt as if there were no other way to talk. To look back is to remember people arguing about issues great and small (long after the canonization of bebop) and to remember how fans absolutely had to have a position on everything. East Coast "hot" (say, Clifford Brown) as against West Coast "cool" (say, Chet Baker). The Apollonian approach of the Modern Jazz Quartet as opposed to the Dionysian approach of the Art Blakey quintets. The so-called third stream. The Lydian Method. "Free" playing. Fusion. Acoustic versus electric. And so forth and so on. My point is not to make a complete list, but to show the pattern, the long history of arguing and nitpicking.

In part because of all this posturing, jazz fans have often not known what was happening even as it happened around them. (Some players, too, for that matter.) As a teenager, I went to one of those extravagant Carnegie Hall jazz shows—one group after another for hours—specifically to hear Charlie Parker. (Claude Hopkins, an important dance-band leader in Harlem, had told me about Bird while giving me a free piano lesson in the basement of an old Dixie club called Stuyvesant Casino.) Backed up by a small string section, Parker played like a demented angel— but he was billed seventh or eighth; few in the audience knew of him and fewer still listened with more than half an ear.

Perhaps ten years later, I was part of an ongoing jam session in the downstairs bar of a club on Eighth Street in the Village. One night, the owner approached me as I was getting up from the piano. "You should listen to the guy upstairs," he said. "You could learn a lot." (Downstairs was a walk-in bar; upstairs was tablecloths, waiters and a cover charge—this last waived for musicians, as was the custom in those days.)

I did indeed go upstairs, and what I heard there drastically, almost violently, opened up my understanding of what might

be possible in jazz. It was possible to voice chords without playing the roots. It was possible to play an entire tune without a
dominant seventh and the kinds of cycles that flow from dominant sevenths. A great deal could be accomplished by implica-
tion; one didn't have to state everything, or play all the notes of
a given scale or chord. That which was left out was sometimes
as important as that which was included. I listened to the trio
for three nights, and for most of the time I was an audience of
one. Too overwhelmed to talk to the musicians myself (they
seemed a bit standoffish in any case), I nevertheless tried to get
some of the funky-blues musicians from downstairs to come up
and check it out. They'd listen to a tune, or part of a tune, and
then leave. "Cocktail music," they said. I had thought so too, but
only for the first five minutes. The trio was Bill Evans, Scott La-
Faro and Paul Motian, in what I believe to be Evans's first New
York gig. No one came to hear them, and the heartbroken
owner had to let them go.

In some senses, having fans can be worse than not having
them, worse at least for the musician who is trying to reconcile
the music being played with the feedback from those listening
to it. The Beat Generation took up jazz with enthusiasm. Kerouac, Corso, Ginsberg et al. prowled the jazz clubs listening to
bop musicians and praising the emotional spontaneity of their
solos, the freedom from constraints of form. They believed the
"wild" sounds were direct, unfettered expressions of raw emotion—some kind of animalistic, ejaculatory jungle music. They
were unaware of bop's grounding in Bach and its continuation
of the reconciliation of chromaticism and tonality, let alone its
neo-Baroque, rule-ridden severity. So intent were the Beats on
co-opting jazz into their abject romanticism they did not hear
the music. Like so many others, they patronized, projected and
did not hear.

· · ·

If you go to the jazz section of your local record store and pick randomly, you will get mostly music based on two short forms —the blues (usually, but not always, a twelve-bar structure) and the ballad or tune (usually, but not always, a thirty-two-bar structure). Ballads or tunes that are especially interesting harmonically, and are thus worked over by successive generations of players, become what are known as standards. "Going to Chicago" is a blues. "Autumn Leaves" is a standard. These forms are short and quite simple. Their simplicity becomes a virtue because it allows for greater latitude in improvisation. The original tune means little in jazz; it is the variations that count. For example, if we consider "I Got Rhythm" (a standard) as the theme, we quickly notice that the thousands of variations played by hundreds of jazz improvisers offer pleasures well beyond the original tune. The theme becomes a sub-subtext and often is not even heard or recognized by nonplayers.

Many jazz musicians have also created original short-form tunes without lyrics, structurally similar to blues and standards, and written lines (melodies) and done improvisations based on those tunes. Horace Silver comes to mind. Others have taken the harmonies (chord changes) of popular tunes and written lines over them completely unrelated to the original melody, a practice that was economically, if not artistically, inevitable since melodies can be copyrighted and chord changes cannot. Charlie Parker was a master in this regard.

It has been a great delight to witness the breathtaking inventiveness with which the short forms have been explored and continually revived. Thelonious Monk's use of space, Coltrane's exploration of modal scales, Sonny Rollins's architectural structures, Bill Evans's exquisite voicings for piano, Keith Jarrett's pressurized metrics, Miles Davis's artful elisions, Paul Desmond's musical wit—the work of these musicians and many others suggests that the short forms will always be appropriate for jazz and that the challenge of making music with them and within them is, for all intents and purposes, infinite.

Blues, tunes and ballads had the advantage of fitting the 78 rpm format used in homes and jukeboxes. Short forms were also in demand on the dance floor and on radio and thus dominated jazz during a large part of the music's history.

Even with the advent of the long-playing record, larger forms were only rarely explored. Those musicians who did move in that direction, despite economic disincentives, were acting for artistic reasons, feeling, one assumes, that a natural pressure existed inside jazz that might allow for an expansion of the music.

In 1940, Artie Shaw wrote his *Concerto for Clarinet* with a commission from Hollywood, two sections of which have been released on CD. Section one is a crisply orchestrated B-flat blues, but section two is something else altogether. Shaw wrote blocks of ensemble music and then improvised solo clarinet in such a way as to leave one block, make a solo structure and enter the next block of tutti like a man jumping from one ice floe to another. Improvisation is a basic element of jazz, but this was a new way to use it—improvised solo lines to connect discrete harmonic structures. (Major symphonies have recorded the work; the clarinet soloist reads the transcribed notes of Shaw's original improvisations!) The second section is short in duration, but a definite statement of Shaw's inclination to move the energies of jazz beyond the twelve- and thirty-two-bar forms. His early retirement from the big-band scene was due in part to his inability to find support for that experiment.

In 1943, Duke Ellington recorded *Black, Brown and Beige*— an extended work for jazz orchestra, forty-five minutes playing time, that drew from jazz conventions while taking on the challenge of longer than normal forms. Ellington, often working with Billy Strayhorn, is to jazz music what Shakespeare (according to Harold Bloom) is to Western literary culture—a colossus.

His influence can be clearly heard in artists as diverse as Thelonious Monk and Bill Evans, or the big bands of Gil Evans and
Woody Herman. Ellington laid down a foundation so strong
that its use went in all directions, from the a cappella group
Take Six to Dave Brubeck. His compositions, harmonies and
part-writing are so important that one simply cannot do any
significant work in jazz without having absorbed them.

Fans, critics and musicians may argue about everything else,
but no one would deny Ellington's centrality to the canon. He
had ambitions for the music—the early big works like *Black,
Brown and Beige, Diminuendo in Blue / Crescendo in Blue* and
other compositions leading him inevitably toward the sacred
music (as he called it), a kind of post-jazz experiment that preoccupied him during the later years.

There is a point at which orchestration ("the charts," in Jazz-
speak) passes beyond being a technical matter and is better described as composition. That happens when the work is so
fresh, persuasive and powerful as to break new ground. Elling-
ton-Strayhorn, for example, followed by Charles Mingus.

As a young man, Mingus played with Charlie Parker and
took part in creating the paradigm of bebop. He worked most
of his life doing combo work, first as a sideman and eventually
as leader of a series of small groups. In contrast to some other
leaders who tended to create a certain musical identity or style
and then stick to it—superb players like Art Blakey, Horace Silver, John Lewis—Mingus was always in motion, pressing the
edges of what was possible with five or six players.

He took chances, changing tempos, using dissonance, shouts,
stray sound effects, unfamiliar harmonies and whatever else he
needed to wring every ounce of musical juice out of whatever
tune, blues, riff or ballad he played. That was how he made his
living. At the same time, he was writing, creating post-Ellington
compositions that both contained the master and opened new

territory. *Duke Ellington's Sound of Love* and *Open Letter to Duke,* for instance. After Mingus's death in 1979, it appeared that much of his more ambitious writing would never be played again, but that has not, happily, been the case. His magnum opus, *Epitaph,* a two-hour piece of great power, was performed in its entirety, for the first time, at Lincoln Center in 1989. The piece is big, fiercely intelligent and written in such a way as to allow for the active participation of the players through improvisation. The orchestration *is* composition, but space is left for the instantaneous composition of others, so that no two performances will ever be exactly the same. Thus, the melding of jazz with what might be called the non-string symphony is achieved. Evolution.

Following on Mingus, we have Wynton Marsalis. Classically trained at Juilliard, jazz trained with Art Blakey's Jazz Messengers, Marsalis was the first to win a Grammy for both jazz and classical recordings in the same year. At thirty-four, he is the leader of the new generation of jazz artists. He discovers young talent; they play with him, form their own groups and discover young talent who play with them, etc., etc.

It is a pyramid that grows broader and taller every year, an accessible and educational structure whose reach now spans the country. His combo work, using the short forms, has been fresh, original and extremely sophisticated, but he has also been writing long forms—ballet music (as did Copland), an extended work called *Citi Scape* and other strong pieces.

The world premiere of *Blood on the Fields* at Lincoln Center in 1994 marked the symbolic moment when the full heritage of the line, Ellington through Mingus, was extended into the present. A secular oratorio in twenty sections, *Blood on the Fields* presents a narrative about slavery in the old South. A speaking chorus introduces each section, and the work is scored for jazz orchestra and three singing voices. Marsalis researched the music being played at the time and refers to it with great deftness. The result is a contemporary piece laced with the flavors of blues, marches, church music, turkey in the straw, Dixie and more. It also reflects a full awareness of Copland and Stravinsky. The libretto is earnest, veering between prose and poetry, but the music is powerful—rich and constantly surprising. Somewhat more than Ellington and somewhat less than Mingus, Marsalis includes improvisation and spontaneous participation of the players in the grand design. He moves his harmonies and shifts his keys in ways that seem natural and yet never predictable (making great demands on the singers: "It's hard," Cassandra Wilson, the lead singer, told me. "You're between keys sometimes").

Blood on the Fields is also a convenient marker for the transcendence of the old classical jazz / modern jazz schism. The new generation of jazz players and composers feel free to draw from everywhere, the more sources the better. Dixie, Bartók, bebop, regional music—all grist for the mill. Marsalis grew up in New Orleans, and those sounds are in his ear, but so are many others. What is important about his writing is that it demonstrates how jazz conventions and jazz "feel" can retain and renew energy while expanding into large forms that contain other elements and other traditions. Jazz need no longer be marginalized, neither in its structures nor in its emotional and intellectual ambitions. It is, after all, music.

At the recording sessions of *Blood on the Fields,* Marsalis stands on the podium facing the brasses and reeds. To his left, the piano; behind him, the drums and bass. Everyone can see him clearly, even the singers behind glass in semi-soundproof booths above and behind the trumpets and trombones.

Microphones are scattered about, wires running this way and that, taped to the floor; rugs are hung over lampshades or two-by-fours as acoustic baffles; sheets of music spill from folding chairs, and the scene seems, at first glance, to be somewhat chaotic.

Marsalis is of medium height, with a large chest and a round face, but there is something in his physical appearance that defies direct description. A kind of stillness or rootedness to his frame. He seems to fill space more densely than other people somehow.

He raises his arms, counts off the tempo almost under his breath and the room is filled with sound. His conducting technique (no baton, of course) is spare. Crisp, minimal movements to make cues, adjust dynamics or indicate endings, which he does by holding up his hands, palms together, moving them apart as the sound rings and then making a little flourish at full extension for cutoff and silence. He indulges in little hip swings, little shoulder drops or head noddings when the music moves him. Mostly what he's doing is listening, listening with great concentration. He is loath to stop the band and does it only when he has to.

"Hey, stupid," he says affectionately to one of the saxophone players, who looks about seventeen. "You are off-key. You are flat. What's happening?"

The boy mumbles something about his reed and, head down, fools with his mouthpiece.

"Well, fix it up, little brother," Wynton says lightly. "Make that reed behave."

More than half the musicians at the session are in Marsalis's touring group or the groups he has used for recording. The rest are particularly fine players, both black and white, with the interpretive and improvisational skills Marsalis wants.

The prevailing mood at any rehearsal or recording session is quite important, affecting both the efficiency of the use of time and the quality of the music being played. Marsalis is very, very good at setting an informal yet highly professional tone while the work is going on. When the time is right, there is a good deal of banter—teasing, jokes, etc. (The white trumpet player making moues to his black colleague, trying to crack him up while the reeds play a long section, for instance. Okay as long as it doesn't go too far.) There is a tangible sense of affection, of warmth between the musicians, including Wynton, and a sense of pride because they are all members of an elite group. It isn't difficult to imagine that every man in the room feels a sense of personal authentication from the company he is keeping. Certainly there is a total absence of cynicism and very much a sense of the band working wholeheartedly together in what they clearly feel is a worthy endeavor.

The band staggers to a halt when the bass trombonist breaks off in the middle of a solo. Marsalis understands.

"Okay, okay," he says. "I heard it. But don't lose the low harmonics you got on the B-flat this time. I liked that texture." He raises his arm and they start again.

There are only a few odd sheets of music on Marsalis's stand. He works from memory even though the oratorio is almost three hours long. (Two flights upstairs, listening through headphones, the producer has the full score.) He also works quickly —if a line isn't correct because of an error in the transcript or interpretation, he will lift his head and simply sing it in a strong voice to indicate how it should go. He has the ability to communicate rapidly with his players and singers, talking about timbre one minute, call and response the next, or getting across subtle issues of shading, tone, color and the like as if by telepathy. It is a pure joy to watch him work.

Lunch break. Marsalis has no sooner stepped down when the sound engineer is at his elbow with some technical matters. The producer appears two minutes later for a brief huddle. The players are getting up, stretching, drifting out to the hall where Sony has laid out a buffet of sandwiches, finger food, cakes and salads. A cheerful mood prevails.

Wynton takes a seat beside me. "You want to eat?" he asks. "There's a Japanese place down the block." He leans back, and it's clear he doesn't want to leave immediately.

"I know it sounds pompous," I say, "but I think this is a historic piece of music."

He smiles and looks at me. "Thank you, man." After a moment he says, "Take a look at the libretto when you get home. You write; maybe you can teach me something."

I indicate the empty bandstand. "These guys are terrific. That part toward the end, where you've got the two trumpets playing a minor second against each other? They didn't waver. No vibrato, just solid."

"Yeah. That jazzy sound. I love it."

"So many great young players coming up now. A whole new wave."

"They got a ways to go before they catch up with the old guys, though. Don't know how to play slow; don't know how to play soft. Crazy about velocity. Well, velocity by itself don't mean a thing."

I nod and drop the matter. Marsalis has high standards, for himself as well as everybody else.

Now, in the studio, we look across the room where Reginald Veal, Marsalis's bass player, is running through the score for a tall, skinny white kid who I later learn is a student at Stuyvesant High. Reggie plays a long sequence while the kid watches his fingering, they converse for a moment, and then the kid tries it. This goes on for some time.

"Who's that?" I ask.

"He's from a master class. And look, there he is getting a free lesson. Why don't they write about that?" Somebody wants Marsalis and he springs out of his chair. Eric Reed is at the piano, quietly playing some bell-like chords. I go over and we chat about them. He's written the sequence quite recently.

Ten minutes later, Wynton seems ready to go to lunch.

"Did you see the tune of Eric's?" I ask. "Nine bars forward and then you play them backwards?"

His eyebrows go up and he turns and goes to the piano.

Eric stands and Wynton sits down and looks at the music. He plays through the tune, then returns to a three-bar section that he plays several times over. Without the melody line, the score indicates D-flat 7 (flat 5/flat 9), G-minor 11, F-minor 11, E/G-flat, A-flat major 7 and E-minor 9.

"So is that a resolution?" Eric says from over Wynton's shoulder. "Technically?"

Wynton turns his head away from me and speaks to Eric. I can't catch what he says. He plays a quick series.

"Yeah, okay," Eric says. "I never did understand how that worked. I'm thinking of fixing it up to do on the road." And then, almost apologetically, "You know, for club dates."

Now, in this perfectly ordinary moment, I felt a click of recognition, a sign of how profoundly the world of jazz has changed. It was the subtle apology, the tacit understanding that although club dates were worth doing for reasons both musical and economic, they were no longer the apex.

For a long time, playing the A clubs across the country was, along with recording, the ultimate goal. The final brass ring. That is no longer the case. Eric Reed, a young and brilliant jazz pianist, along with his whole generation, knows in his bones that the music is expanding, growing in scope and ambition, and that the future will involve a great deal more than club dates. Combo work has become a test and a rite of passage toward a grander enterprise. What used to be the end, in a certain sense, has become a part of the beginning.

"Let's go eat," Wynton says. And we do, taking the kid from Stuyvesant with us.

1995

The Serkin Touch

I'M VERY INTERESTED in technique," Peter Serkin says as he goes to the piano. His tone of voice conveys a quiet relish, as if to say that interpretation is paramount, but the immediate, practical questions of physical technique are more fun to talk about. "I like to keep my hands right on the piano, the fingers touching the keys all the time—or as close to it as the music allows—and you don't have to sacrifice dynamics." To convince me, he rests his fingers on the keys, plays a very loud chord, releases the keys without breaking contact and then plays the same chord softly. He listens. "They say Chopin had ten thousand separate degrees of pianissimo," he says with a quick glance. Serkin's control of pianissimo is one of the first things a listener notices in his recordings.

His hands are ordinary-looking hands, the fingers a bit thick. Watching him play a very loud chord with very little movement, it occurs to me that perhaps they are thick because they are strong. They would have to be exceptionally strong to do what he does with forte. "Yes, you can keep finger contact with the keys. There's even a thing you can do"—he hesitates—"after you sound the chord; you can make it a little louder and longer."

"What?" This would be magic.

"Look under there, at the hammers." He strikes a chord,

holds the keys down and then somehow milks the strings with infinitesimal pressure conveyed to the hammers, extending the chord without sounding it again. "I shouldn't be showing you this," he says good-naturedly. "And if you do it this way, you can make the chord degenerate faster than it otherwise would." He strikes the same chord, holds the keys down, milks the strings at a different rate, and the chord implodes, folds into silence. Magic. A trick passed down the line of great teacher-players, a trick that only a great player could possibly execute, given the exquisite degree of finger control needed to bring it off.

What it means to be a great pianist is much more complicated now than fifty or sixty years ago, when everyone knew the eight or ten players who had the full repertory, the technique to play the repertory and the emotional depth to interpret it. Fifty or sixty years ago there were simply fewer brilliant players, particularly in terms of technique. If the eighty-eight keys of the piano can be thought of as a filter, not many people got through in those days. Today there are hundreds upon hundreds of technically dazzling pianists, and to find the best, one must go past the body of the music to the more difficult question of the soul of the music. And it is there that we find Peter Serkin.

"Many players just play," one professional told me, a man who attends four or five piano events every week during the season (and who must remain anonymous). "In fact, a surprising number of them just play. Serkin always has a point of view of his own. He has an interpretation that reflects his character. When I hear him—no matter how familiar the piece—my emotions have been altered. I don't know how to explain it. You believe him. He's really there. It's like when Edith Piaf sings a song about some bruiser beating her up and throwing her out in the alley—you believe it because she really knows about those emo-

tions. If a Judy Collins sings it, it's empty. Many pianists working today are empty. It's like they never grew up, never had anything happen to them."

Serkin was three years old when he became aware of the
power of music. At that time, one imagines, he realized that
music—which had surrounded him always—was separate from
him, other than him, outside, as it were. Living in Vermont in a
musical family, he heard music all the time. His mother played.
His father, Rudolf Serkin, one of the greatest pianists of his generation, was away a good deal, but when he was at home he
played. Guests, visitors and his parents' friends played. Peter's
infancy and young childhood were so infused with music that it
must have come as a shock for him to discover that, unlike sun-
shine, air or his bucolic surroundings, music was not elemental.
It had to be made. One imagines him thinking, before the age of
three, that the music was playing the grown-ups. When he discovered this was not so, he wanted lessons.

"Nobody pushed me—not then and not later," Serkin says,
sitting in the living room of the small apartment he shares with
his second wife, a photographer, on the Upper West Side of
Manhattan. This seems to be an important point for him. He
was a child prodigy, but he wants to make it clear that choice
was involved. His own choice. Nobody forced him. Serkin is a
tall, pale man with a handsome face that rarely changes expression. A cool face. When it does change, the changes are subtle.
His eyes are faintly Asiatic and rock-steady behind his glasses.
He seems a careful man—friendly, thoughtful, perhaps even
cautious. There is a sense of controlled tension, of watchfulness.

He taught himself to read music, and he learned quickly, becoming a first-rate sight-reader while still a young child. (Sight-
reading—the ability to play anything put in front of you on
sight—is a specialized skill, which need not necessarily be connected to other talents. There are plenty of sight-readers who

play the piano as if working at a typewriter, without emotional involvement.) For Serkin, sight-reading was a way in, a means to discover and get closer to the music of one composer after another. He played everything he could get his hands on in a house that must have contained most of the piano literature in print and thousands of other scores. And if he already sensed the power of music, now, through his continuous active sampling of the masters, he began to perceive something of its form.

His childhood was a bit lonely, he says. Vermont was remote in those days, and the very wide spread of ages among his siblings, with Peter somewhere in the middle, was another factor. And at school, he remembers, "everybody would run out."

Serkin was nine when his family moved to Philadelphia. His father had been going back and forth from Philadelphia to Vermont for years, but his increasing involvement with the Curtis Institute of Music, and the Philadelphia Orchestra under Eugene Ormandy, motivated the shift. Peter kept on sight-reading. "My parents would hear me playing all sorts of stuff. They'd say, 'You should be doing scales.'" He smiles. It is clear he is fond of his parents.

At the remarkably tender age of eleven, Serkin entered Curtis, which was to provide his general education and his broad musical education. He began playing professional concerts and recitals at the age of twelve. At fourteen, he began to study piano with his father.

"I was terrified of concerts," he says, taking off his glasses and rubbing his eyes. He replaces his glasses and leans forward. "I used to throw up before concerts." From outside come the shouts and yells of children playing in a nearby schoolyard, shrill sounds of controlled hysteria. "I was a very neurotic kid, I think."

Yes, perhaps he was. The pressure and tests he faced before, during and after adolescence were possibly more arduous than even he can explain. He was also the son of a famous father who was also one of his teachers. Because he was a prodigy, he was somewhat isolated within his own generation. He describes himself as having been very serious, a little old man, and what remains unspoken is that he may have expected too much of himself. At seventeen he was making enough money to support himself, and after graduation he moved to his own apartment. A year or so later he got married, then had a child. Soon after that he gave up music.

The decision to stop playing—and at Serkin's level that's what it had to be, play or don't play, with nothing in between—must have involved a great deal of pain, to say the least. It was a passive repudiation of his entire life. Serkin does not talk about the decision now, except to say it happened. He mentions in passing his concomitant confusion about what was going on at the time —a bad war (Vietnam), civil strife and so on—as if to help explain the constant traveling that he began doing in 1968. The central reason, however, must have been because he wasn't going to play anymore and he needed to retreat to some distant, private place in order to put himself back together again as a new, nonplaying person. In the winter of 1971 Serkin moved to Mexico. With his wife and baby he lived a simple life in a town almost totally devoid of the accoutrements of culture. Eight months went by.

"One Sunday morning," he says, "the radio was on in the house across the way. It was Bach, and as I listened it became clear to me that I should play. The whole question was simplified somehow." Serkin stares into the middle distance for a moment. "I had to give it up in order to discover it." He looks at me calmly, and I get the feeling he is wondering if I can understand. I also get the feeling he doesn't care that much—he has told me the truth, in the simplest possible form, and the rest is up to me. Despite his reticence, I find myself thinking of the event in Mexico as the central one of his life, with all that came before leading up to it and all that followed flowing from it. He does not describe listening to the Mexican-radio Bach as a mystical experience—characteristically, he does not analyze, he simply states—but it is hard to avoid thinking of it that way.

Barely into his twenties, he came back and started all over again. "I did scales," he says, "and enjoyed it. I didn't know what to expect after all that time not playing, but it was fine." As he began studying with various people, his development as a mature artist commenced, and his professional life recommenced. He made records, appeared as soloist with the great orchestras and played solo recitals. By the late seventies he was generally ranked as one of the top two or three pianists in America, and one of the top ten in the world. Many of the new generation of musicians rated him higher. Indeed, Serkin had reached a level of excellence—both in playing and in interpretation—where ranking becomes difficult, if not meaningless.

Significant in Serkin's rise was his avoidance of competitions. (Nor will he now act as judge.) Some might say it was easy for him to stay out because he was well connected already, but this sounds unduly harsh. All the way through he seems to have made his choices for aesthetic rather than practical reasons. Competitions, he would say, are relevant in athletics but not in art. Chamber music began to interest him during this period, not only aesthetically but also because playing it was less lonely than solo work. In 1973 he formed the chamber ensemble Tashi (Tibetan for "good fortune"), which had slightly unusual instrumentation and a collective interest in contemporary music. Indeed, his championing of some modern composers of whom he is especially fond—Messiaen, Toru Takemitsu, Peter Lieber-

son, Stefan Wolpe and others—has in itself set him apart from
his peers, and has required tough-mindedness and a certain
amount of risk. Concert producers in general like to avoid new
music, but Serkin has continued to program new music into his
solo and chamber recitals, and over the years important record
producers who got too involved in what he should play and
how he should play it have watched him go to small labels that
leave him alone.

The American composer Ned Rorem says of Serkin: "His
uniqueness lies, as I hear it, in a friendly rather than an over-
awed approach to the classics, which he nonetheless plays with
the care and brio that is in the family blood, and he's not afraid
to be ugly. He approaches contemporary music with the same
depth as he does the classics, and he is unique among the super-
stars in that he approaches it at all. He is the only big name of
his age to feel a duty toward the music of his time."

Serkin doesn't like to talk about his career—a word he dislikes—but seems genuinely to have been thinking all the while
about music, with the assumption that his career would take
care of itself, as indeed it has. Money doesn't interest him. "I just
never paid much attention to it," he says. Beyond meeting his
responsibilities to his extended family, he doesn't think about it.
His rent-controlled apartment is furnished simply, with two
Steinway baby grands, a wall full of music, and a new hi-fi his
wife gave him to replace the antiquated little setup he'd had
since his student days. He has the slightly abstracted air of a
man who did not so much reject materialism as fail to notice it
in the first place.

Serkin plays all the time in the house. He calls it playing, not
practicing, and he enjoys it. He will also be working on whatever project is current, because that is his method. To take six
Mozart concertos and completely immerse himself, for example. Or the *Goldberg Variations,* or whatever. This intense work

has to do with locating the music he will eventually play for the public—going over a piece in the most painstaking detail, taking it apart and putting it back together. His way of doing this is not set, but rather varies from piece to piece. "In the old days I was somewhat more methodical. I'd take the left hand, for instance, and work on that alone. Then the right hand alone. Then together. Now I'm somewhat freer. I listen. I try to be responsive to what I sense are the intentions of the composer." It is this penetration of the score that constitutes Serkin's real work. Nothing is taken for granted, no matter how familiar the piece. (Indeed, the more familiar the piece, the more pressing the need to examine it.) "When I prepare a piece, I go back to square one," he says. "I'll do all sorts of things. If the score indicates accents on the second and fourth beat of the bar, I'll try putting them on the first and third. I may work on a bar or two for an hour, if I feel there's stuff in there. I'll vary the tempo. I'll even change the time signature—see how it sounds as a waltz." He unravels the music, in other words, and looks at it from different angles. Presumably this activity helps Serkin get past his awareness of how other people (Horowitz, Rubinstein, Schnabel and others) have played the piece and discover how he wants to play it. It is from this work that his interpretation springs—and when the critics describe him as profound, or deep, or words to that effect, it is the end result of this kind of work they are describing.

Serkin thinks of himself as an American pianist, and although he is very much a modern player, to whom the nineteenth-century mannerisms of the previous European-trained generation seem a bit fusty, he is aware of himself as part of a tradition. "I studied with Horszowski," he points out, "whose teacher was Leschetizky, who studied with Czerny, whose teacher"—the briefest pause for emphasis—"was Beethoven." He speaks of his teachers with great affection—particularly

Horszowski—even if he did not always agree with them.

"Casals was a wonderful player, of course, but some of his teaching was pretty crude: the idea that if a run of notes goes up, you should play louder as you go up, and softer as you go down. I don't see why that should be true." Even an untrained listener can hear what Serkin has been able to do through his rejection of this old popular idea. When he plays long single-note runs, they do not seem, as they so often do with the older players, to be aimed at the last note. They do not lean forward, and hence their shape seems clearer somehow, and they never seem rushed. Many great players have used a sort of quasi-biological vocabulary, words such as "breathing," "pulse," "tension" and "release," to describe what they do, to describe the mode within which their interpretation will occur. Serkin goes at playing differently, and one senses that he doesn't want a mode of any kind unless it emerges from his analysis of that particular piece. It might be breathing, and then again it might not. He has a stubborn independence about these matters that must sometimes have tested the patience of, say, Pablo Casals. But of course he has prevailed, and he is very much aware of it.

Serkin's style is self-effacing; Serve the composer, his motto. He dislikes self-indulgence in a performer—dramatic body movements at the piano, finger painting in the air and so on, strike him as distractions. "Some of them talk about cutting through the orchestra. I don't want to cut through them, I want to play with them." The whole bravura style, the attempt to dominate the music, is not what he is after. He wants to release the music. "It all depends on the piece. Sometimes you can tell [the composer] wants to make a splash, wants to shock, even, and so you play it that way." He is also disappointed in what might be called the homogenized style—a bland, official kind of approach. "A lot of what you hear on the radio," he says, gesturing to the hi-fi, "is just dull. It just runs on without a whole lot of feeling in the playing."

Having extended his control over the piano to the point where the question of whether the music he plays on it is outside him or inside him seems no longer a relevant one, Serkin now gives more attention to the practical details of his professional life. "I'm managing myself," he says. "I really enjoy concert work now, but I was doing too much. You fly in, play with stuffed-up ears, fly out, play again. City to city. I'm going to pace it better. I think I'll play better."

As much as he has already accomplished, a great deal of music lies ahead of Peter Serkin. How might he play Debussy, for instance? Which contemporary composers emerging now will catch his ear? The direction his future development takes will be both important and fascinating, wherever he goes. Whatever devils he may once have had, he is free of them.

1985

Hip Vaudeville

ON THE OUTSKIRTS of Newburgh, New York, a sad, tattered city quietly going to ruin on the banks of the Hudson, is Stewart Airport, an old army air base recently taken over by the Metropolitan Transit Authority. In that more or less deserted airport is an enormous airplane hangar, where old signs—"RECON," "OPS"—hang askew over peeling door frames, and in which the Rolling Stones have constructed the special portable, monstro, lotus-leaf stage for their American tour.

Why Stewart Airport? Because the whole place is fenced in with the barbed hardware of military security, constantly patrolled by MTA cops, and because the Stones can fly in from Montauk on Long Island and step directly from their plane onto the stage. Why rehearse in an airplane hangar? Because the light ring suspended over the stage weighs six tons and the sound equipment floating thirty feet in the air weighs about five—enough load to bring down the roof of an ordinary building. And, of course, for space.

Four complete steel bands from a single West Indian neighborhood in Brooklyn. One hundred steel-band players with their wives, girlfriends and children, pouring out of trucks and buses onto the tarmac, pushing their bulky instruments in rented wooden carts, smoking joints, playing soccer, tapping cowbells and dancing in the waning sun. The leader of one of the bands explained that all one hundred of them would be in the New York show at Madison Square Garden. "We're de warm-up for de show," he said. "We keep everybody hoppy till the Rolling Stones begin to play."

As darkness closed in and the Stones, who should have arrived at six P.M., still hadn't appeared, the bands moved their instruments into the hangar and set up on the concrete at the foot of the high, tilted, eighty-foot stage. One hundred black people scurrying around under the gleaming altar, staring up over their hand-hewn drums at a quarter of a million dollars' worth of instruments shining at the center of the lotus, fixing sliced rubber balls under the bottom rims of their fifty-five-gallon bass cans. Above, a technician sprays the keyboard of a Rhodes electric piano with an aerosol mist and wipes the brightwork with a clean chamois. As if to reassure themselves, the West Indians begin to play.

A great wash of sound fills the building. One would swear there was an organ playing underneath all the percussion—some unimaginably huge roller-rink organ gone recklessly native. Standing outside the echoing hangar, one hallucinates string sections and choral groups, so dense are the overtones. The Stones' airplane (prop-driven on this occasion, not the big jet) lands and taxis up to the hangar without anyone hearing it. One by one, trailing birds and bodyguards, the various members of the most famous rock band in the world drift inside, and the steel-drum music continues unabated.

Mick Jagger, nearly thirty-two, his small, perfectly proportioned body clad in close-fitting pants and a simple cloth jacket, takes up a position in front of one of the black bands. He stands quietly among the onlookers, smiling, apparently pleased with the exuberant music and the striking visual effect of the players. (The steel drummers, who promise to be a *coup de théâtre* in the Garden, were his idea.) Lead guitarist Keith Richard, thirty-one, strides across the room, all loose and gangly, scarves flowing, shirt billowing, a fat, stylized urchin's cap pulled low on his narrow head, his arms flapping as he does a little dance. He disappears behind a curtain in the back of the hangar. Bill Wyman, thirty-two, and Charlie Watts, thirty-seven, respectively bassist and drummer, and the only other original Stones, enter unobtrusively and melt into the crowd.

Although seven musicians are playing in the band on this tour, the point is made that only four of them are Stones. The other three are described as guests (Billy Preston, keyboard, and Ollie Brown, percussion) or as a temporary replacement (Ron Wood, backup guitar). These distinctions have to do with what has come to be called image—apparently quite important.

When the steel bands have finished, Jagger meets with the leaders and his British stage crew in a small office ("DEBRIEF") to discuss arrangements for the Garden. Jagger wants steel drummers below the lotus stage, surrounding it on all sides, and he wants fifty more players.

"Fifty boys that quick," one of the leaders says, shaking his head slowly. "I don't know, mon. Maybe."

A British stage manager strokes his beard, gazes thoughtfully at his pendant belly and raises his head. "There's a spice problem, Mick. The drums are big. We have to think about spice."

"It'll work." Sitting on a bench, curled puppylike against the huge chest of one of the blacks, Mick stabs at a map of the Garden. "Here and here. All around. You can do it." He fields a few questions from the black leaders, who would obviously like to keep him there as long as possible, going over everything two and three times; then he suddenly loses interest and leaves. The blacks follow.

"Oh, dear," the stage manager sighs, picking up the map. "Bloody nogs with their bloody great tins. Bloody marvelous."

Stones rehearsals are casual affairs, more like unhurried, attenuated, stop-and-go jams (except for the lack of improvisation) than polishing sessions. If something goes wrong in a tune, the players just gradually fade out one or two at a time, peeling out of formation, and eventually there is silence. They wander about the stage, talking, smoking, drinking a bit or jiving around until someone starts playing (usually Keith, occasionally Charlie), and then begin again. It may be the same tune, or another. The hiatus may have been five minutes or an hour. Technical discussions of the music are both brief and rare, since the tunes are fairly rigidly set or fixed, without room for variation. And since they've played most of them for years, there would not appear to be a great deal to talk about, except perhaps sound levels or various electrical questions in connection with their instruments.

There is a feeling in rehearsal that rather than doing focused work on the music, the players are concerned with re-establishing physical intimacy with their instruments. Between tours and record dates, there are extremely long layoffs (compared with those of most professional musicians), and despite practice at home and occasional guest appearances it seems reasonable to assume that the Stones need a good chunk of time before a tour to get their individual chops back. To prepare for the current tour, they've been living together for a month in advance, playing six or seven hours a night, in their rented house at Montauk.

Onstage at Newburgh, the Stones play one or two tunes for the blacks, who then move out, back to the buses and trucks for the long ride to Brooklyn. The Stones had planned to stay only a few hours, to familiarize themselves with the stage, but they become intrigued with the acoustical properties of the hangar and wind up staying all night. Their loud, driving sound is emphasized by the sonic brightness of the building. But the volume is so loud and the echoes so thick it is hard to hear anything distinctly. The amplified Yamaha grand is inaudible most of time, no matter where one stands, including onstage. A great deal of Charlie Watts's lighter cymbal work is lost in the fuzzy blare of the guitars. Upper-register notes from Wyman's bass fail to materialize in the ear. It is a kind of soup of sound dominated by Keith Richard's guitar echoing and re-echoing back upon itself.

Jagger, relaxed, bops around the stage, eating a sandwich, occasionally grabbing a microphone to shout out a tune in short phrases, sipping a beer, swinging his beautiful little girl's butt in time to the music. He is a fantastic dancer, even when he's dancing small. There is an astonishingly expressive range in his moves, a mysterious eloquence. The gestures are clean and clear, one instant saucy, the next haughty. He offers, he takes away, he prances, poses and preens. He changes character in the blink of an eye with a precision one associates with pantomime. But, above all, he is a tease. His consummate artistry as a tease is what drives audiences wild. *Come and Get Me* is the name of his dance, and he is sufficiently beautiful so that men, women and children, teased long enough, eventually reach the point where they want to climb up there and eat him alive. They want to sink their teeth into pert, outrageous little Mick the way they'd go at a piece of honey-fried chicken. Jagger is aware of this, and plays to it. It is the basis of much of what he does onstage, and a good deal of what he does offstage. (The representations of Jagger's art as some kind of satanic celebration of brutality are misleading. The net effect of his dancing, at least, is quite gentle. He is a tease, and if he stands for anything, it isn't rape but *coitus interruptus*.)

The rehearsal at Newburgh goes on all night. Production

crew, grips, electricians, carpenters, truck drivers, lighting crew, security people and a few privileged hangers-on mill around listening to the music. By five or six in the morning, most have drifted away, back to the motels of Newburgh to get some sleep. The Stones and perhaps a dozen of their friends stick close together onstage, gathering in the central sunken portion during breaks for refreshment and a bit of privacy. Dawn breaks and they play on. At nine or ten in the morning, they pack it up and fly back to Long Island.

The estate is on the tip of Long Island, facing the sea. It once belonged to Princess Radziwill, who sold it to Andy Warhol, who rented it to the Rolling Stones. The security gate is manned by a hip young black—Afro, blue jeans and beads—who checks his lists and lowers the chain. A large German shepherd lunges at the car and stops in midair, brought up short by his leash.

The driveway meanders past several outbuildings and cottages up to the main house—a large one-story clapboard building looking out over the water. A Bentley is parked by the front door. Two scruffy young security men sit in the sun near the kitchen. Another German shepherd, tied to an enormous log, barks furiously.

"You gotta watch the dogs," one of the young men says. "I don't trust them myself."

Inside, the house appears to be deserted, but after a moment a slightly chubby, friendly, unmistakably working-class Englishman emerges to lead the way into the living room. This is Stu, friend, adviser, protector, factotum and occasional piano player ("Brown Sugar") to the Stones. He explains that people are just waking up and should be coming along soon (the time is four-thirty in the afternoon). He offers drinks and cigarettes and disappears into another part of the house to answer the telephone.

Instruments dominate the room: a beat-up grand piano, trap

drums, congas, timbals, guitars, microphones and amplifiers. Everything is set up and properly placed, waiting to be played. At the far end of the room, a black leather couch and matching armchairs cluster around a screened-in fireplace. Other than that, the place is bare. A few books lie about—Dashiell Hammett, some science fiction and a hardcover copy of Rona Barrett's autobiography.

In the kitchen, a tall English girl bustles back and forth, putting a meal together. "Ah, well," she says good-naturedly, "you can't worry. The other day I made a gumbo, took me hours, and then they go order a pizza. All those lovely shrimp gone to waste. Not to worry, though." When asked about the difficulty of cooking for people who keep the sort of hours the Stones are famous for, she replied, "You never know is the thing. You might have a roast ready and then they want breakfast. Scrambled eggs. You never know." Cheerful, slightly dazed, she goes to work on a buckwheat salad, chopping herbs and tossing them in the bowl. The sound of music in the living room. One of the security men is at the piano playing some fairly good jazz— Monk and Ellington—and suddenly Charlie Watts appears and goes directly to the drums. A wiry man, almost gaunt, with hair cut so short the shape of the skull is clearly discernible. Large, expressive eyes dominate his face. He jumps right into the music and plays light, swinging jazz drums for more than an hour, until the pianist runs out of tunes. Toward the end, Watts tries some double-time effects, superimposing related time signatures over the basic four-four of the piano. He plays well, and seems happy as he comes off the stand, wiping the sweat from his brow.

"That was fun," he says. "I haven't done that in a long time."

Keith Richard crosses the room on his way to the telephone. "You do like that jazz, don't you?"

"A running joke," Charlie explains as Keith disappears. "I'm the only one that started with jazz. They all came out of rock, and they tease me a bit." Relaxed and affable, Watts sits on the couch with his feet on the table. "We've been here a month. It's like the army." He corrects himself. "The Boy Scouts: get up, play, go to sleep, get up, play." He talks about Parker, Zoot Sims and Coltrane, all of whose work he admires. He chats about jazz in England during the early 1960s—Ronnie Scott's old club and the various big bands with which he's played. An obviously intelligent man with a fine, laconic wit, he seems unaffected by his celebrity, speaking his mind openly without a trace of guardedness. When asked if he could hear the other musicians in the hangar, or if he can hear them in large concerts, he answers without hesitation. "No, to be honest." How does one play, then? "You play with the people you can hear. It changes from moment to moment and from place to place."

The girl from the kitchen comes in to find out if Charlie wants anything special with his dinner, and he jokes with her in working-class argot, sending her into a fit of giggles. He throws up his hands in mock despair. "Think what the man's going to write. Even the cook laughs at him." He wanders off to take a shower.

Keith Richard is the musical center of the Stones. His lead guitar dominates the proceedings, and it is he who writes the tunes, runs the rehearsals and decides all things musical. When he talks about the Stones, he seems to have worked out in advance exactly what he wants to say. He speaks quickly, wasting no time, and although his remarks are concise, informative and to the point, one senses that he's a bit tired of it all, tired of having to respond to endless questions. "The writers from the rock press are all so deadly serious," he says. "They interview me as if I were Stravinsky. It's absurd."

He seems relieved that there are no tape recorders or steno

pads in evidence on this occasion. "Mick's leaving was a bit of a shock"—Mick Taylor, former backup guitar with the Stones, gone to form his own group—"but I can understand it. At his age, he should be playing all the time. With the Stones, there can be eight or nine months at a time without anything much going on. That isn't good for a young player. Ron was the natural one to take his place. He'd played with us a lot. Mick was a soloist, really. Ron is a bit more fluid."

In response to a question about the degree of improvisation in the Stones' music, he says, "There isn't any, really. The music is fixed. But there's still a certain amount of give-and-take"—presumably in terms of dynamics and meter—"and then there's Charlie. I don't know what we'd do without Charlie. What's special about him is the fact that he can swing, and, you know, most rock drummers can't. They haven't got the touch." He stops talking and stares off into the middle distance, as if he'd just remembered something. One is struck by the signs of age in his face; like Jagger, he has the body of a boy and the face of a forty-five-year-old man. He leaves abruptly. Characteristically, he moves fast, jumping up and running off with great loping strides. He is a preoccupied man.

Jagger, the tease, has promised a long walk on the beach, drinks and dinner (through an intermediary, to be sure), but none of that occurs. He is with Warhol, in one of the other buildings, being photographed. Stu explains that Warhol is trying to get him to pose nude, but that Mick isn't having any of that.

A splendid meal is served in the kitchen at sunset. Pasta with a meat sauce or clam sauce. Buckwheat salad and mixed greens. Pan-fried steaks. Three or four varieties of cheese, including a really good Brie, wine, beer and a large platter of fresh fruit. People come and go, helping themselves, sitting anywhere. Skinny Charlie Watts fills his plate three times. Plump Stu can't finish a single helping. One of the security men complains in a whining tone that he isn't going to get to go on the tour. "It isn't fair," he says. "I'm the one who's been doing all the work." No one seems to know what to tell him.

At midnight, Jagger, Richard, Watts, Wyman and Wood gather in the living room. (Preston and Brown are in California for a couple of days.) They tune up, adjust levels and begin to play. In the small space, with the volume high but not distorted, everything can be heard. Almost immediately, they find a solid groove and nestle into the sound, like men warming themselves at a fire. Structurally, the music is simple to the point of being primitive. There are few chord changes, sometimes only two or three—and no modulations. What holds the music together is the phrases—short, melodic and rhythmic figures which can be tricky, and which must be played with absolute precision—and the beat, the warm, taut beat with that special energy and power for which the Stones are justly famous. If the music in the hangar had been hazy, it was not so in the living room. Tough, driving rock, with all hands getting it on, it is irresistible music, music that makes you feel good right down to your socks. Jagger responds, and begins to sing. Bobbing and weaving, pumping the mike at Ron Wood, he sings in his own voice, an amalgam of countless black American singers cooked in the head of a British mimic. He does several choruses in a lovely, perfectly controlled falsetto, and laughs as the tune ends. Spirits are high on the stand as they decide on the next tune.

"What key is that in?" Jagger asks, picking up his guitar.

"I think you'll find it's in R," Wood says in the arch tones of the BBC. "The key of R."

They play all night long and into the morning.

The opening concert of the tour is at three-thirty P.M. (the crack of dawn, as it were) in the Assembly Center at Louisiana State

University. Seating capacity, 15,000. As the doors open, the kids, their mean age twenty-two or -three, pour in and rush to fill the open space around the stage. Near the barrier, they stand fifteen or twenty deep, gazing up at the lotus. Farther back, they sit on the floor or promenade around the hall to watch each other. In the distance, the banked seats of the auditorium are gradually filling up. Outlandish dress and outrageous behavior are at a minimum. The crowd seems indistinguishable from any gathering of kids from any small city in the South. Many of them wear T-shirts with the logos of different rock groups printed front and back, presumably souvenirs of previous concerts. Except for one kid trying to crash without a ticket (chased, caught, pulled out of the hall by his hair, handcuffed and arrested by a large policeman), everyone is well behaved. They listen to a local group called the Meters, applaud generously and wait patiently for the Stones, who finally appear onstage an hour behind schedule. The audience roars.

With a blaze of light and a great onrushing wall of sound, the show begins. Stage, lights and sound have all been designed to project the show over vast distances, to somehow enlarge and expand the musicians and carry their images to the farthest seat in the highest balcony. A half-million watts of electricity is the lamp, the Stones are the film, and the audience is the screen. In terms of visual phenomena—Jagger's dancing, the dipping, swaying movements of Richard as he plays, the pumping limbs of Watts on percussion, the color, sparkle and flash of the set— the show is highly successful. Everything can be seen, and seen clearly. The sound is another matter. The music is blurred. The piano is once again barely audible—which is particularly disappointing, since Preston is such a superb player. There is a beat, to be sure, and the kids are clapping their hands happily enough, but the music is not precise. In the living room at Montauk, there were times when the Stones seemed to be floating six inches above the ground, held aloft by the sheer tension of the rhythm; here, they are only playing. (Very different conditions, and perhaps comparisons are inappropriate, but it does seem strange that the Stones in concert allow the sound level to go so high they are effectively prevented from playing their best, solely to project what they do play to the most distant customer.) The point of the concert is Jagger—not the music. The music supports Richard's guitar, and Richard's guitar supports Jagger's singing and dancing, or, more to the point, Jagger's presence. The opening concert is low key, but the kids love it.

During the break before the evening concert, the Stones have to deal with the press. Very few media people have been granted access during the previous month, but now that the tour has officially started, reporters descend from all directions. Charlie Watts sits alone on a bench outside the pressroom-cum-hospitality-suite, perhaps loath to enter.

"A nice audience," he says. Asked about the lack of new tunes on the program, he says, "Of course they like the old favorites. They like to hear the tunes they know. We'll work some new stuff in gradually." A general discussion about playing large concerts follows. "They're not really concerts, are they?" he says. "It's a show, a sort of theatrical occasion. It's theater."

Inside, Mick Jagger is being interviewed by Geraldo Rivera under a bank of TV lights. A chatty exchange of small talk. Jagger is immensely charming—his charm alone carries him through without the need to say very much or reveal very much. He appears to be enjoying himself.

Billy Preston is told that the piano was inaudible. "It's going to be different in each hall," he says quickly. When asked if he could hear the others, he evades the question.

Bill Wyman answers the same question directly: "No, I couldn't." Wyman is an interesting figure. He has a quick mind and a sly playfulness which blends well with Watts, who often plays his foil. Onstage, he stands perfectly still, laying out an impeccable bass line. If Jagger comes over and mugs in front of him, facing him, a few feet away, Wyman stares out over his shoulder as if nothing were happening, as if nothing occurring onstage had anything to do with him. Offstage, he gets plenty of sleep, doesn't seem to take anything stronger than champagne and, in every way, gives the impression of the mature, balanced man at peace with himself and the world around him.

When asked if Jagger, in concert, provides a visual tempo cue for the players, he laughs outright. "Don't be silly. He doesn't always move in tempo. You couldn't trust it." Wyman deals patiently with the press and then goes off and plays Ping-Pong. Rivera wants to interview him, but he declines. Rivera moves camera and lights across the room and films himself playing Ping-Pong with Wyman, who wins the game forthwith.

At the evening performance, it becomes clear what's going on. Jagger is indeed the point, and the music becomes no more than the frame for his performance. The music may be good ("It's a rush to go in front of all those people," a rock performer once said in another context about Carnegie Hall. "The energy can get you off. It can make guys play up a storm under the worst conditions"), or the music may be mediocre, but the audience is only half listening. They are digging Jagger's moves.

One thinks of the melodramatic stage of the nineteenth century, the music hall and the silent films. Jagger knows how to reach a large crowd with the sorts of gestures and stylized movements one associates with those forms. If the word "sleep" is in the lyrics, he will place his hands together, slip them under his cheek, close his eyes and bend his body downward to act out the concept exactly as it would have been acted out before the age of electricity. He can move as a clown moves in the center ring of a circus, expressing surprise with measured, exaggerated care. He can blow kisses from the edge of the stage like a turn-of-the-century diva. In this sense, he is a modern practitioner of an almost forgotten art. Young people who have never seen anything like it before, since nothing like it is on television, are swept away. Add pantomime, the delicious tease of the *Come and Get Me* dance, the modern jive moves, the sexuality of the mouth, face and body, and his acute stage sense, and you begin to have Jagger. What he does is a hip version of a vaudeville act, and of course vaudeville was once very big.

Afterward, the reporters collar whatever Rolling Stone they can. The questions are perfunctory and oddly lifeless. People seem to be struggling to find something significant to ask, and the thought occurs that there really isn't much to talk about. Can it be true? Twelve and a half million dollars anticipated ticket gross. Huge auditoriums all over America selling out in a matter of hours. It must mean something. The American Zeitgeist, sociological trends of youth, aesthetic brutalism, drug use, modern sex, narcissism—all of these must work in somehow, but there is no way to frame the questions and no one to answer them. There are simply seven young men playing music, men who don't know anything more about the Zeitgeist than the people who come to hear them.

1975

Observations Now

I THINK MOST PEOPLE who attempt to write with a degree of seriousness are curious about others doing the same thing. Writing is a lonely enterprise, after all. Some seem comfortable in the mental solitude. I think of writers I've met over the years—Graham Swift, John Updike, James Salter, Marilynne Robinson and others—who appear to be unbothered by what might be called the isolation of work, the necessary isolation involved in the act of working. They seem suited to it, although in every other respect they are quite different, as writers and as people.

I am uncomfortable writing, and I know a number of writers (although I won't mention them) who feel the same way. The isolation, self-doubt, perfectionism and other idiosyncratic impediments to action—some completely irrational, almost like superstitions—mix in various ways in various people to create something close to dread at the sinister urgency of the blank page. For myself, once I'm up and moving, if not running, through the lines, I zip back and forth between feeling okay and feeling terrified. Once in a while I am exhilarated, but more often it is as if my inner self, my sense of myself, is at risk. Something like the tension one might feel watching the ivory ball circumnavigate the roulette wheel after having made a large, foolish, impulsive bet.

I imagine F. Scott Fitzgerald as a kindred soul. I'm not thinking of the quality of his work, of course (dreadful at its worst, genius at its best), but of what I take to be his underlying state of mind—a tense mixture of manic energy and deep unease. I believe it was there long before his breakdown.

The term "nervous breakdown" is currently out of fashion, but I allow myself to use it because that is what I used, several years after the fact, to describe to myself what happened to me as I finished my autobiography thirty-five years ago. I've never written about it, in part because I don't think I can adequately describe it. Indirection is the best I can do. A fear of consciousness itself, fear of myself, beginning on a single afternoon when the sky fell (Chicken Little was right!) and continuing for a number of years of panic and struggle. My condition became my life, and in those days there were neither pills nor any appropriate theoretical models of brain function to help explain what was going on. I could only, out of shame and great effort, hide the inner turmoil, put on a mask of normalcy and soldier through one day at a time. It was a close thing. A very close thing.

Such an experience puts an end to innocence. Fitzgerald describes it well in *The Crack-Up*. Eventually he was able to write again—*The Last Tycoon*—and pick up the thread of his unique take on the world. His strength and courage in the face of adversity are more moving to me than Hemingway's love affairs with death. I actually learned something from Fitzgerald, and it helped me get out from under, as they say. As sentimental as it might sound, or as presumptuous, I think of the man as a brother. I believe I know him.

2001

Great Scott

A T THIS POINT, it's not easy to read Fitzgerald straight, to simply take in the work as it stands on the pages. So much has been written about his life, so many anecdotes, reports, stories and (no doubt) fantasies have been bruited about over the years that our attention is constantly veering back and forth between the individual man and that which he managed to create. This happens to some extent with all important writers, but the problem, if that's what it is, is particularly acute in Fitzgerald's case, partly because of his writing methods and partly because his life was melodrama on a grand scale.

I knew nothing about the man when I first read him. I was a teenager gobbling up books indiscriminately, working up the shelves of my dead father's library. There was a distinct sense of having struck gold when I reached Fitzgerald. I was reading over my head, of course, but nevertheless there was a special and weirdly inexplicable feeling of having found a kindred soul, a fellow romantic, a fellow outsider trying to find a way into the realm of beauty and power, where, one supposed, people lived lives of much greater richness and depth than one's own. Intelligent, spiritually energetic, Fitzgerald seemed dedicated to an exploratory quest, a journey into the vast magic of the world where astonishing events would occur and important discoveries would be made. As a skinny, lonely kid in almost constant emotional pain of one kind or another, I wanted to believe in this vast, magic world and the possibility of escape into it. I felt the yearning in Fitzgerald immediately, although it took many years for me to realize the full scope of it, how very much was yearned for, including, perhaps, death itself.

It was the pressure of the restless, searching soul behind the prose that pulled me in. But it was not long before I became aware of another, extraliterary undercurrent going on in the newspapers, in conversations and in the culture having to do with the man himself. Not about the writing but about the man. To be famous in America in the first half of the twentieth century was a different experience from what it is today. Famous people were understood to be permanently elevated to a high plateau of society, to have, in a certain sense, passed over into another life. Fitzgerald was especially fascinating to the popular imagination because he was understood to have fallen. (Others have fallen, but not so publicly, so noisily.) An irresistibly attractive romantic, tragic figure to the hoi polloi and their cruel attentions, Fitzgerald produced a body of work that was eclipsed by the swift appropriation of his life into a cautionary fable.

The best biography is Arthur Mizener's necessarily rather dark study, *The Far Side of Paradise,* a humane, thoughtful book that manages to stay calm and sympathetic while enumerating the relentless cascade of catastrophe and bad luck—so extreme as to seem almost Greek—that marked Fitzgerald's short stay on earth.

Briefly then, F. Scott was born on September 24, 1896, into an unremarkable middle-class family of Irish origins in St. Paul, Minnesota. He was bright, lively, but not particularly popular as a boy. When it was time for college, he picked Princeton on a whim, spent most of his first two years writing musical theater, going to parties, trying desperately through one route or another to become a big man on campus and avoiding all forms of work he found less than amusing. Not surprisingly, he eventually flunked out. He joined the U.S. Army, served briefly within the confines of the United States and was about to be shipped overseas when World War I ended and he was released. (One can't help wondering what avenues the experience of battle might have opened in his young mind. Would he have been shot for cowardice, as his traitorous friend Hemingway once remarked, or would he have pondered the power of ugliness with at least a fraction of that energy with which he worshiped the power of beauty? Who knows? Certainly not the ever-posturing Ernesto.)

Without money or clear prospects, girl-crazy Fitzgerald had lost his first love and seemed destined to lose his second, a southern belle named Zelda Sayre. But he was still very young, full of optimism and extraordinary energy, and having decided toward the end of the Princeton years that he wanted to be a "great writer," he went to work and wrote, and then revised, under Maxwell Perkins's direction, his first book, *This Side of Paradise*. It is at this point that we can in retrospect begin to see the overt-good-news/covert-bad-news pattern of so much of his life. *This Side of Paradise* was a great popular success, making him rich and famous almost overnight. But the book was juvenilia—high-spirited, fresh, with occasionally wonderful writing, but in many ways a mess. Formless, glib, intellectually sloppy, superficially trendy, it had no depth and only the faintest hints of the power and seriousness that would eventually emerge in his work. Nevertheless, it was the book that made him, that identified him as the chronicler of the jazz age, flappers, gin, flaming youth and new money. He was "fast," as the age was "fast," and he was to pay dearly for that reputation for the rest of his life. The good news was that Zelda married him;

the bad news was hidden in her genes. She was as Blake's sick rose, and the invisible worm was on its way, big time.

Scott Fitzgerald never seemed to doubt that he could make his living writing, with no other sources of income. The speed with which he spent every cent of his very considerable earnings through the twenties suggests an assumption that his future was secure. The Fitzgeralds were restless people, renting enormous houses, traveling, staying at hotels, tearing through Europe, and everything had to be first class. They spent money faster than he could make it and were always on the edge, most often in debt. His main source of funds, it should be explained, came not from his novels (*The Beautiful and Damned*, 1922; *The Great Gatsby*, 1925) but from the short stories he wrote for the *Saturday Evening Post* and other magazines. In that era, the major magazines were highly influential. The *Post* had a circulation of more than two and a half million. It was an American institution, with the power, for instance, to make Norman Rockwell a national icon. Through its pages, Fitzgerald became the best-known short story writer of his time, being read by millions of people who probably didn't know he wrote books and probably wouldn't have bought them if they had. At his peak, Fitzgerald earned what would be today about $25,000 for a short story—and he wrote plenty of them. Three times more than Hemingway. But again, he was being rewarded for work that was not his strongest. In the short form, he wrote perhaps a dozen masterpieces ("Babylon Revisited," "Absolution," "The Diamond as Big as the Ritz," "The Ice Palace," among others), stories that will last forever, but he also wrote a hundred that have been forgotten, most of them deservedly so. It was commercial work, hard work, and it took energy—energy, it is easy to say now, that might better have been saved for more serious endeavors.

This, after all, was the man who wrote *The Great Gatsby*, a short, elegantly constructed novel destined to enter the canon. Virtually every American novelist carries the book around in his or her head.

That Fitzgerald managed to create it in the midst of the most manic decade of his life stands as proof that he was much more than the charming, clever, impulsive, spoiled, alcoholic boy-man of popular image. He had the power and the courage to embrace severe discipline. He had the ambition to aim high. He was profligate, to be sure, but he was also deeply serious. (The good news: by 1980 *The Great Gatsby* was selling 300,000 copies a year. The bad news: in the 1930s, when Fitzgerald was still alive and in desperate need of money, *Gatsby* sold roughly 700 copies a year.)

Poor Zelda. If she'd married some nice, solid, stable young man from the cotton exchange and lived the quiet life, she might have been able to slow her inevitable decline into madness. (Her family was shot full of it.) As it was, she married a manic-depressive, half-mystical, financially irresponsible progressive alcoholic who unknowingly sped it up. One facet of her sickness was ambition, powerful ambition—but in the abstract. By that I mean it had no object, no route. Scott wanted to be a "great writer," in part because he responded to the external force of literature. Zelda wanted to be a writer (she was uneducated) or a dancer (her teacher, EGOrova—my capitalization) or a painter, not because she had been informed by those disciplines but because she desperately wanted to be a great something. She shared with Scott a powerful drive toward self-authentication, but she lacked a route. Thus she never matured. She remained a girl, utterly dependent on her husband and pathologically jealous of his talent.

In spite of their romantic image and the hyperbolic love-besotted tone of so much of their correspondence and public remarks to each other, Scott and Zelda are hard to take seriously. As youngsters they were in love with love—a common enough place to begin—but their relationship didn't seem to go anywhere. They fell into a complex *folie à deux* of role playing, cross-identification, alcoholic escapism and denial.

We have Fitzgerald's work, in any case, in which his treatment of women may well have been driven by personal psychology in addition to artistic strategy. His female characters are mostly girls—fresh, spirited rich girls, beautiful in conventional terms—who are important not so much for what they are as for what they stand for. The king's daughter, the old-money heiress, the golden girl. They are symbols of a mystical and dimly understood otherworld to which Fitzgerald was drawn, as a Catholic monk might be drawn to the other reality of Heaven. His girls are angels, wounded or otherwise, complete with halos. They are to be adored rather than loved.

One of Fitzgerald's great strengths as a writer was his ability to make this metaphysical beauty believable, to have us feel its power. It amounted to an obsession, and it dazzled him. Halos dazzled him. The kind of frisson felt by a man who marries a plain woman, lives, grows and changes with her through the years, and then one day happens to be watching her through the windows out in the garden clipping flowers, and for no reason at all suddenly sees a feminine beauty in her so deep it almost takes his breath away—to this kind of experience, this kind of love, Fitzgerald was numb. Or uninterested. There was something androgynous about the man. (I do not mean he was gay or anything along those lines.) Something of the mystic.

Gatsby (with its mistreated angel, Daisy) was a great critical success. T. S. Eliot wrote, "In fact it seems to me the first step that American fiction has taken since Henry James." But the book did not sell. As the twenties drew to a close, Zelda grew sicker and the medical bills mounted. Still, they went on with hotels, servants, nannies for their child, trips, champagne and the high life in general. Scott poured out the short stories to pay for it all, knowing he was "whoring" and beginning to resent it. The crash of 1929, which occurred while the Fitzgeralds were living in France, had little immediate effect on them, since they owned no stocks and had no savings. Scott continued to get top dollar for his stories through 1931. Zelda's first hospitalization was in 1930. (Most of the rest of her life was spent in various expensive institutions.) Scott no doubt thought that the publication of *Tender Is the Night,* in 1932, would bring in pots of money to cover everything, but that was not the case. The book did not sell.

The Depression changed America. It was deep, and it was almost unbelievably long. Hollywood distracted the people with fluffy movies about gay, rich sophisticates and with opulent musicals in which everyone danced, burst into song and fell in love. But the literate public in those days expected more from books. They looked for good questions, if not answers, about the miserable reality into which the giddy American Dream had collapsed. Neither the critics nor the readers could see past the surface of *Tender Is the Night,* whose characters do no work, spend a lot of time on the beach, worry only about themselves, care nothing for politics and are awash with nostalgia. To be sure, it was easy to assume the book was an extension of the otiose, spoiled nonchalance of *This Side of Paradise* and the glittering, moneyed landscape of *The Great Gatsby* with its endless parties. Anyone who read the gossip columns knew that Scott not only wrote the books but actually lived that life with his deliciously wicked flapper wife. The irony is that *Tender Is the Night* does indeed pose good questions, deep questions, about decadence, spiritual confusion and loneliness. It is exquisite social satire. Fitzgerald knew perfectly well what he was doing, but because of his reputation, few people could believe it.

Tender Is the Night is a multilayered work of the imagination, a created world and not, as it was first perceived to be, a history, a "chronicle." The author's method involved using bits and pieces of his own experience, bits and pieces of people he knew and situations he had seen, lived or noted, to get started and to create a narrative arena. There is a difference between history and fiction, and Fitzgerald's interest was fiction. He squabbled with Zelda about the use of raw materials from their years together. He wanted to protect the fictions he might create from being identified with the histories, memoirs or chronicles Zelda (who could do no more) might assemble. He was right to worry, since many critics still thought of Fitzgerald as a chronicler and read him accordingly.

The game of identifying Fitzgerald characters—Nicole from *Tender Is the Night is* Zelda; Abe North *is* Ring Lardner; Monroe Stahr in *The Last Tycoon is* Irving Thalberg—becomes irritating because it is reductive and misleading. Fitzgerald was not trying to capture specific people; he was trying to create fictional characters, complete with souls, and he used a sort of gross matrix of situations and dilemmas that he had observed in real people as a way to begin sketching his own made-up people. To identify Nicole as Zelda is to miss Nicole (and Zelda as well). To misrepresent Fitzgerald as a social historian is to miss his great achievement as an artist. Unfortunately, all of this happened. More recently, the Fitzgerald revival and the careful attention of literary critics has helped clear the air.

Scott Fitzgerald's decline occurred rapidly. The man who had brought such fantastic (albeit manic) energy to his work, to riding around on the tops of taxicabs drinking champagne, to his doomed marriage—this man found himself out of gas. A number of factors contributed. He was not just an alcoholic; he was a *gonzo* alcoholic. (At one point in the early thirties, he decided to cool out, and he gave up gin, allowing himself only beer. He would start at breakfast and drink thirty-six before bedtime.) The alcohol damaged his frail body and fucked up his mind far more than he ever seemed to have anticipated. The money had stopped coming in as magazine readers' tastes and interests changed during the Depression. His wife had gone mad, and he felt guilty, since the kind of life they'd led might have contributed to her disintegration. His best work as a writer was going unrecognized, his journeyman's work in Hollywood was a failure, old friends had turned on him (Hemingway most cruelly of all), and his belief in himself was beginning to falter. Still he wrote.

During 1935 and 1936 he published three confessional essays, later collected as *The Crack-Up*, the most brilliant writings about nervous breakdown (as it used to be called) in our literature. To read them is to understand not the etiology but the subjective reality, the pain, the darkness, the confusion, of a man hitting bottom.

Despite the fact that the author had to write and think in an utterly new and different fashion than he did in his fiction, *The Crack-Up* may well be judged by history to be as significant a contribution as his best short stories. Using the metaphors of spiritual and emotional bankruptcy, Fitzgerald explained the terrifying discovery that the forces leading to his collapse lay in the immutable past. The things done (in all innocence of their power to affect him later), the things not done, invisibly piling up until they overwhelmed the present. A lesser writer might have attempted a specific psychiatric case history, but Fitzgerald was more interested in general existential implications. He was certainly scared half to death; nevertheless, he managed to observe himself, report honestly and teach us a great deal. (This last in contrast to so many of the recent, sometimes elegantly written memoirs about depression that too often seem not much more than a subgenre of travel literature.)

From his breakdown on, we are dealing with a different man. The challenge was not to "recover," as the medicos might say today, if recovery is conceived of as going back to where you were before the trouble and picking up again. One is violently changed by such trouble. For most people, a nervous breakdown, whatever the causes, constitutes the most profound event in their lives, creating such deep changes in their understanding of themselves and of the world that they are forced in many ways to begin all over again.

Scott was $40,000 in debt but still insistent on private hospitals for Zelda and private schools (Vassar, finally) for his daughter, Scottie. There was nothing to do but go to Hollywood. Once again the good news/bad news. Your salary is $1,000 a week, but you'll work with a team on assigned projects. By the time he died, he'd made $88,000 doing hackwork.

In California during his last years, Fitzgerald lived quietly, inexpensively, with Sheilah Graham, a rather vulgar newspaper columnist who looked a lot like Zelda. Instead of running around with glamorous people, he mostly worked on bad movies and also on his novel *The Last Tycoon*. Again the good news/bad news. *The Last Tycoon* contains the finest, richest writing of Fitzgerald's entire career. But he died barely a third of the way through. (Some people say halfway, but if you look at the author's outline, it's clear that it was meant to be a very large book.) And when he died, in 1940, *all* of his books were either out of print or going out of print.

In Jeffrey Meyers's biography of Fitzgerald, there is a wonderful quote from Raymond Chandler about Scott, who he claims possessed "one of the rarest qualities in all literature . . . charm as Keats would have used it . . . a kind of subdued magic, controlled and exquisite." Exactly! Perhaps only another writer could see it so clearly and express it so well.

I would add a few thoughts of my own. Writing is conscious-